WORLD HISTORY

Volume I

FERG#313

WORLD HISTORY

Volume I
The Ice Age to the Renaissance

BY JOANNE SUTER

A Pacemaker® Book

FEARON/JANUS/QUERCUS
Belmont, California

Simon & Schuster Supplementary Education Group

Project editor: Stephen Feinstein
Designer: Terry McGrath
Cartographers: Jean Ann Carroll

Photo credits:
THE BETTMANN ARCHIVE: illustrations and photographs on title page and pages 2, 3, 7, 9, 10, 13, 14, 16, 19–24, 27, 29, 30, 32–34, 37, 40–42, 46–49, 52, 55, 56, 61, 63, 65, 66, 69, 70, 73, 74, 77, 79, 80, 84, 86, 87, 91–93, 98, 99, 102, 104, 106, 110–112, 114, 116–119, 123, 125, 128–132, 135–141, 143, 145–150.

ISBN 0–8224–7475–1

Library of Congress Catalog Card Number: 88–80704
Printed in the United States of America.

2. 10 9 8 7 6 5 4 3
PA

Contents

Chapter 1

Looking at the World's History

Words to Know

A.D. (anno Domini) dating from the year Jesus Christ was born

archeologist a scientist who studies cultures of the past by digging up and examining the remains of ancient towns and cities

artifact a simple handmade object, such as a tool or weapon

B.C. (before Christ) dating from before the year Jesus Christ was born

civilization the society and culture of a particular people, place, or period

culture the way of life—religion, ideas, arts, tools—of a certain people in a certain time

historian someone who writes about the past; an expert in history

Look for the answers as you read:

1. What does history teach us?
2. How do historians learn about the past?
3. Why would anyone want to learn about the people of ancient times?
4. How can archeologists learn about people who lived in the days before writing was invented?
5. Why was life in ancient times just as exciting as life today?
6. Why did people need to make maps in the past? Why do people need maps today?

Temple of Karnac, Egypt

What Is History?

The English fought the Spanish. The North fought the South. One city fought against another. Sometimes history seems like nothing but a long list of wars. But the history of the world is much more than that. World history is also a record of discoveries: better ways of farming, new machines, and new ideas. History is also the story of beautiful art and music. And it is the story of how the people of different times and places lived through hardships. It tells us how they taught their children, looked at death, and tried to explain things that were hard to understand.

History shows us changing times and changing ideas. Long ago, for example, slavery was an everyday thing. The Egyptians made slaves of their prisoners. So did the Aztecs, who lived in a different time and in a different place. But today, people all over the world know that slavery is wrong. A look back at history shows us how much humankind has changed and grown.

Space shuttle

Exciting things are happening in the world today. People go into space. They use the great power of the tiny atom. But were the events of ancient days any less exciting to the people who lived then? What about the day a human being first put his ideas down in writing? Was the first wheel any less exciting than the first rocket engine? People in ancient times must have found discovery and changes to be just as exciting as we do today.

The **cultures** of the past are our best clues to history. By looking at yesterday's people, we can better understand the world as it is today . . . and as it might be tomorrow.

How Do Historians Learn About the Past?

We find out about the people of the past by looking at the things they left behind.

The easiest way we can look into the past is by reading papers and books of days gone by. **Historians** look at old maps that tell how the borders and names of countries have changed. They study all kinds of written records that have come down to us. Then they write books about what they have learned.

But what about **civilizations** from long, long ago? There were times when no one wrote books or drew maps. How do we know so much about the ancient days? People called **archeologists** go digging in the ruins of ancient civilizations. They find **artifacts** that have long been underground. They study each artifact they find. They piece bits of information together. And they come up with a picture of the past.

Scientists have many ways of deciding how old things are. A piece of cloth, an iron tool, a painting on a wall, may all be pieces of the puzzle. And as the pieces come together, bit by bit the story is told!

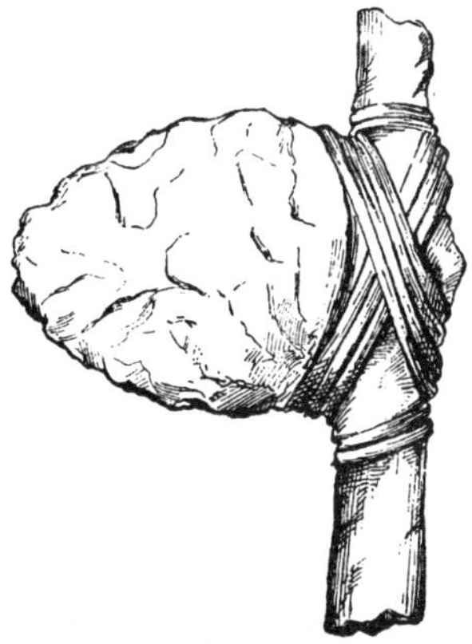

Ancient artifacts

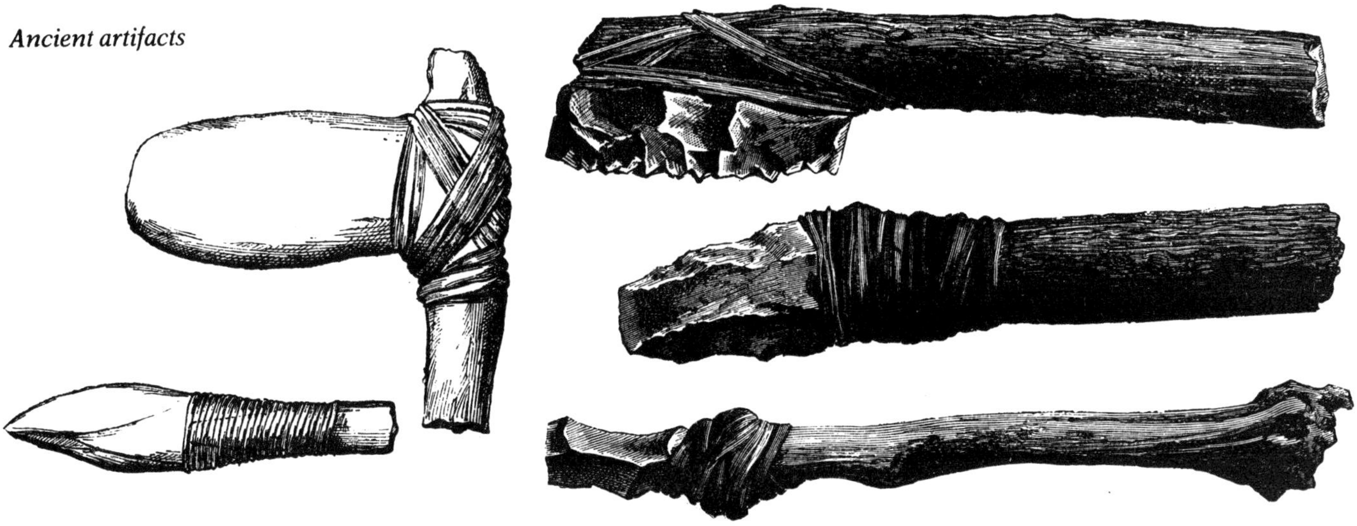

Maps Show the Way

This book has many maps. These maps show how countries have changed, and how groups of people moved. They show that cities were built along rivers and on seacoasts. They show how those waterways made it possible for different people to come together.

People have been making maps for a long time. They drew maps to try to understand their world. And they used maps to find their way from one place to another. Since ancient times, the art of mapmaking has come a long way. Now there are maps to show landforms and maps to show weather. And there are many maps that picture the continents and countries and cities and towns.

But mapmakers have more work ahead. Think about the maps of the future. Will maps be needed to help people find their way among the stars?

The World

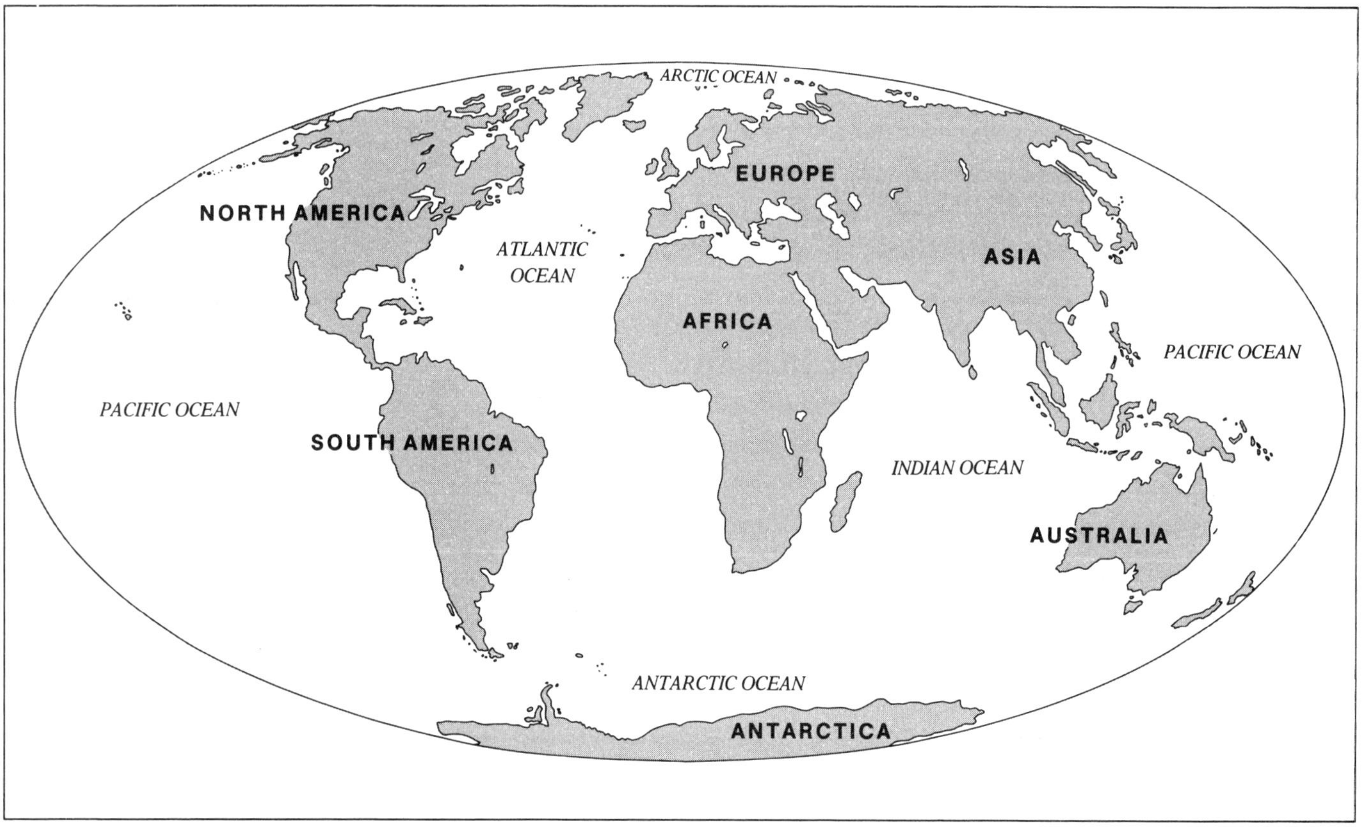

Time Lines

The history of the people of the world is a long and exciting story. The time lines in each chapter will help us keep events clear and in order. Look at the time line on the next page. It gives us some idea of just how long the story is. The chart lists some of the time periods and some of the peoples we will hear about as the story unfolds. If we look closely at it, we should be able to find just where we fit on the time line of history.

It may seem as if some of the civilizations in this book came and went very quickly. But the time line shows that the Roman civilization lasted for about 1,200 years (from about 700 **B.C.** to **A.D.** 500). The Sumerian civilization lasted 2,000 years (from about 4000 B.C. to 2000 B.C.). And the time line shows that the "modern times" section is only about 500 years old. How does the period in history that we call "ancient times" compare in length with medieval and modern times?

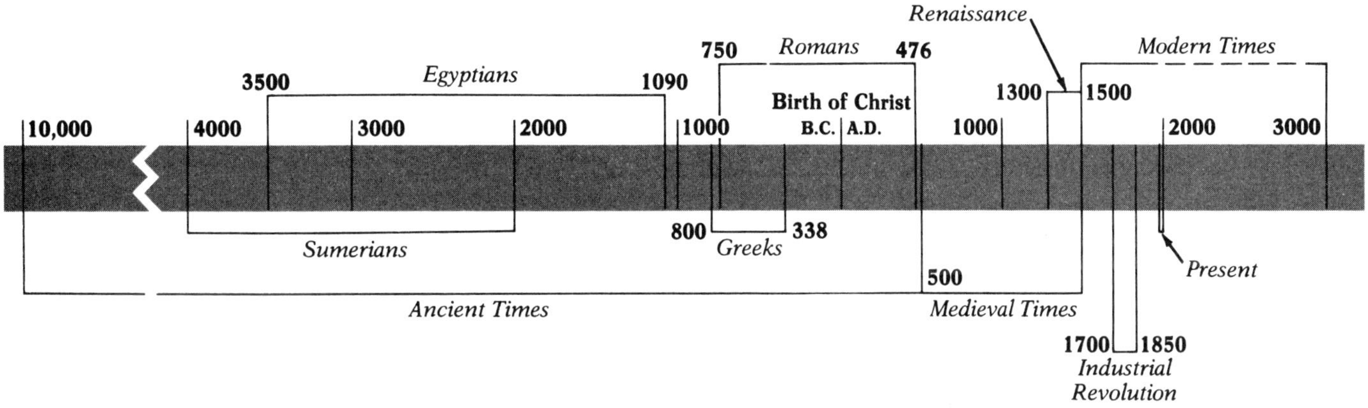

Points to Remember

- ♦ World history tells us not only what happened, but why it happened, what people thought, how they lived, and how they changed.
- ♦ The things that happened long ago help explain the world as it is today.
- ♦ People in ancient times were real people with many of the same worries that we have today.

Think About It!

1. The time line shows us that ancient times lasted for a much longer period than medieval and modern times. Why do you think we know so much more about medieval and modern times?
2. Give two examples of how life today is almost the same as it was in ancient times. Give two examples of how life today is very different.
3. Do you think that maps are just as important today as they were a long time ago? Give two reasons for your answer.
4. What do archeologists do? What do historians do? Do you think it is important to learn about the past? Give two reasons for your answer.

Chapter 2

Early Humans: The Hunters and the Farmers

Words to Know

agriculture the use of land for growing crops and raising animals; farming

crafts a trade or art that takes special skill with the hands

crescent something shaped like a quarter moon

fertile able to produce large crops, as in rich soil

glaciers large, slow-moving masses of ice and snow

revolution a complete change, especially in a way of life or a government

settlement a small group of homes in an area that hasn't been populated

specialize to work in, and know a lot about, one job or field

Look for the answers as you read:

1. What did people learn when the Ice Age ended?
2. How did the development of agriculture change the world?
3. What kinds of jobs did people have in the new settlements?
4. Where is the Fertile Crescent, and why is it important?
5. Why did people start to worry when their villages grew rich?
6. How did the people of ancient Jericho try to protect their town?

The Hunters

Firelight glows on the wall of the cave. It is winter, and the weather is very cold. The ground outside the cave is frozen. But the people inside the cave are warm. They wear animal skins. Their fire, started by striking flint against a rock, is hot. The corners of the cave are dark. But the fire lights one wall. Pictures cover that wall. In the flickering light, the pictures seem to move. One picture shows a man chasing a reindeer. The reindeer is drawn in black. In a second picture the reindeer lies on its side. A spear is sticking out of its body.

There are spears piled in the back of the cave. They are made from strong sticks, bones, and stones. They will not be used until summer. When the ice melts, the hunters will go out again.

Such was life on earth for tens of thousands of years. It was a time called the Ice Age. But this Ice Age was only the most recent one. There were a series of ice ages. They extended far back into the earth's past. During the last Ice Age, the earth's climate was much colder. Most of the world was frozen then. It was covered with thick sheets of ice called **glaciers**. These glaciers had formed in the north. Then they had slowly moved farther and farther south.

In the southern parts of Europe and Asia, the ice melted some during the summer. Little groups of people lived there, scattered about. They were the hunters. They had learned to make simple weapons and tools out of wood and stone. They left their caves in summer to move around. They could not settle down for good. They had to follow the herds of wild animals. They were able to gather some food from shrubs and trees, such as nuts, berries, and fruits. But they mainly counted on animals for food and clothing. Hunting was the most important thing in their lives. Without a good hunt they would die. Just staying alive was very hard for people during the Ice Age.

Cave painting, Lascaux, France

The Farmers

The last Ice Age ended about 10,000 years ago. The glaciers began melting. The land was no longer frozen. People now learned how to grow food. They no longer had to chase wild animals across the lands. Once they learned to raise their own food, they could settle down. That change, from hunting to farming, made civilization possible.

The people of long ago watched the winds blow seeds across the ground. They noticed that new plants grew where the seeds landed. This is how the people learned. They tried planting seeds themselves. They broke up the ground to make it soft. They chose the best seeds, and they grew plants. Next, they made tools to use in farming. They used flint sickles to cut grain and wooden plows to help them dig up the ground.

Once the glaciers were gone, life became easier for people. Now they could count on a ready food supply. Often they grew more than they could eat in one winter. They could store food for the future. They would not have to move away from their homes to search for food. People began to live in **settlements**.

They also learned to tame animals. Some say the dog was the first animal tamed. Next came cows, goats, sheep, and pigs. With their own herds, people had a steady supply of meat, milk, and wool. They now had animals that could live side by side with them. The animals could carry loads and help people with their work.

The Agricultural Revolution

When people began to farm, their lives changed. The change brought about by **agriculture** was very great. For this reason it is often called a **revolution**, the Agricultural Revolution. Now people could settle in large groups, in one place. They chose areas with plenty of water and good soil. They built houses out of whatever materials were nearby. Often the houses were built of mud.

Now the people could plan on how much food to plant each year. They could decide on how many animals to raise in the herds. Now they had more control of their own lives.

Having a large enough food supply and staying in one place gave people spare time. Not everyone in the group was needed to raise food or care for the animals. People began to **specialize.** Some people farmed. Others took care of the animals. And now there were chances to do things they had never done before. People had time to work on their **crafts**. Weavers wove grass into fine baskets. Others made pottery from mud and clay and baked it in ovens. With wool from the sheep, some people learned to spin thread and to weave cloth.

People have raised sheep for thousands of years.

As different jobs developed, so did trading. A weaver might trade his cloth for food from the farmer. A goat might be traded for an ax from the toolmaker. First, trading was carried on within the village. Later people traded from one village to the next.

With the Agricultural Revolution, people's most important needs of food, shelter, and clothing were easier to meet. But now people owned things. The potter had his jars and bowls. The herdsman had his animals. Now there were things to protect! And so people made laws. Most likely a group of the oldest, wisest people in the village would meet. They would decide on rules for the rest of the people.

People started to worry when their villages grew rich. Someone might attack them and try to steal some of their riches! And so people formed armies to protect their villages.

As time went on, villages grew into cities. Later, cities joined together to form small kingdoms. Agriculture is what made this development possible.

The Town of Jericho

Walls of Jericho coming down

The earliest known farming took place along the great rivers of the Middle East. These lands include what are now the countries of Jordan, Syria, Iraq, Iran, and Turkey. This area is called the **Fertile Crescent**. The Tigris and Euphrates rivers provided plenty of water for the land. The soil was rich. The land between the Tigris and Euphrates was called Mesopotamia. That name means "land between two rivers."

Within the Fertile Crescent was the town of Jericho. It is one of the earliest known towns. By about 8000 B.C. Jericho was probably a farming village. Its people built rounded houses of mud and bricks. Archeologists have found remains showing that the people of Jericho buried their dead right under their houses.

The land around Jericho was very fertile. The people grew many crops and became rich. The town grew. Jericho now had to protect itself. The people built a stone wall around their town.

But the wall was not enough. Around 7000 B.C. archeologists say Jericho was probably captured. The houses built after that time were no longer round, but had square corners. This clue suggests that a new group of people must have taken over and settled there.

More is known about the early farming villages of the Fertile Crescent than anywhere else. But farming was developing in other parts of the world, too. By 6000 B.C. farming had spread to Europe. By 4000 B.C. a culture of rice farmers had grown up in China. Between 5000 B.C. and 2000 B.C. agriculture spread across northern Africa.

People began to settle wherever there was good soil and plenty of water. Now they had food and clothing. They had time to learn. Certain cities began to grow into great civilizations.

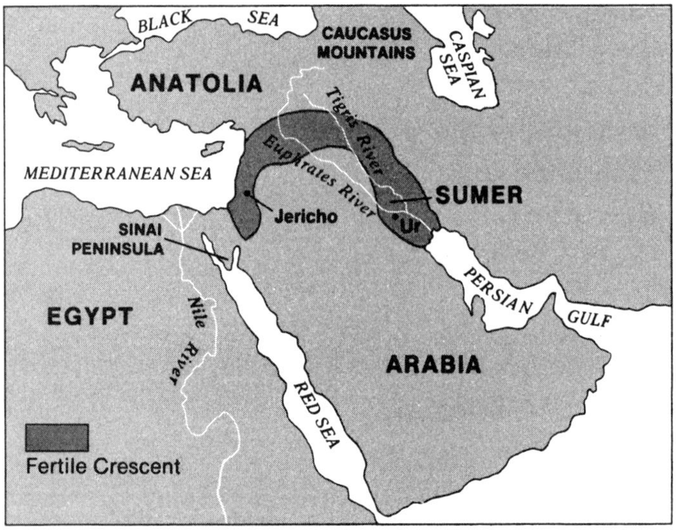

The Middle East: Then

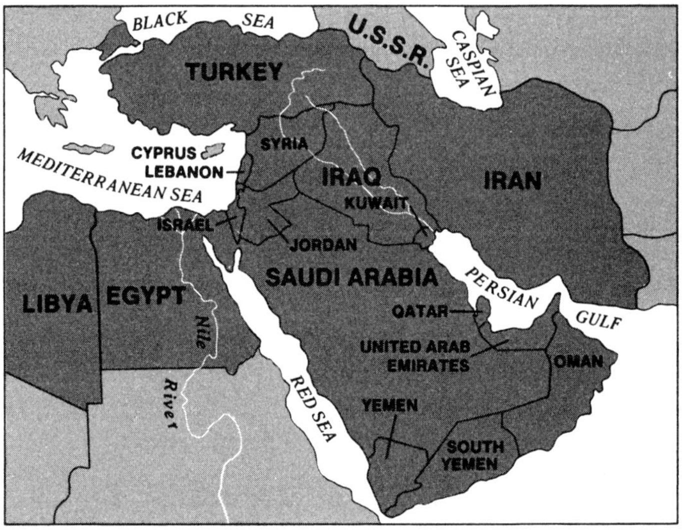

The Middle East: Now

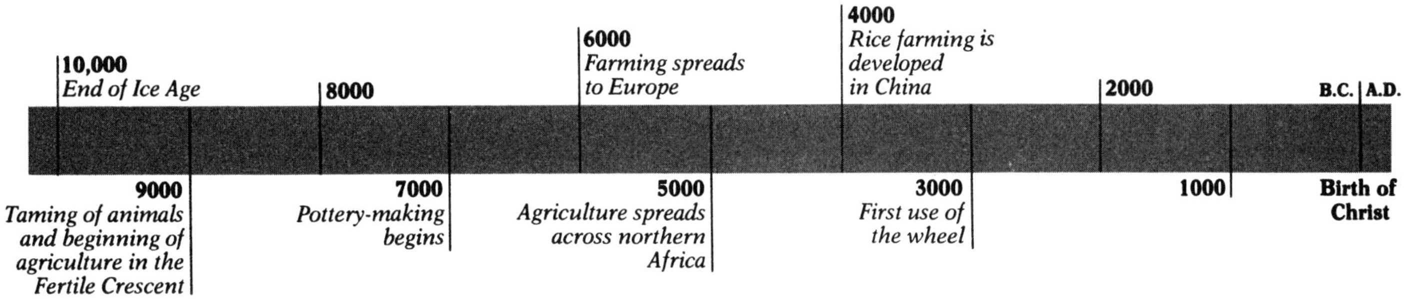

Points to Remember

- During the Ice Age people lived in caves all winter. They hunted for food during the short summers.
- Hunters could not form long-term settlements. They had to follow the animals.
- With the coming of the Agricultural Revolution, people learned to farm land and tame animals.
- Farming meant that people could control their own food supply. They could build houses and settle in one place.
- In the new settlements people had different jobs. New crafts developed.
- Thanks to agriculture, rich cities grew up and trading began.
- One of the earliest areas of farming was in the Middle East, along the shores of two great rivers. It is called the Fertile Crescent.

Think About It!

1. Life was hard during the Ice Age. Give two reasons why you agree or disagree with this statement.
2. Why were people able to invent new things and perfect their crafts after the Agricultural Revolution?
3. Why did the people of Jericho build a wall around their city?
4. Why do archeologists think that Jericho may have been captured?

Chapter 3

The Sumerians: The First Great Civilization

Words to Know

canal a man-made waterway

chariot an open two-wheeled cart, pulled by horses

city-state an independent city and the surrounding land it controlled

contract a legal written agreement between two or more people

cuneiform a wedge-shaped form of writing used in ancient Sumer

dike a wall built along a river or sea to hold back the water from low land

irrigate to bring water to dry land by means of canals

merchant a person who buys and sells goods for profit; a trader

scribe a person whose job it was to write out copies of contracts and other manuscripts. People worked as scribes before the invention of printing.

swamp an area of low, wet land

tablet a small, flat piece of clay used for writing

temple a building for the worship of a god or gods

ziggurat a huge, towerlike temple

Look for the answers as you read:

1. Where was the land of Sumer?
2. What were Sumerian city-states?
3. What did the Sumerians invent?
4. What was daily life like in Sumer?
5. What are the most important gifts the Sumerians gave to the world?
6. Why did Sumer grow weak?

The Land Between Two Rivers

The land that would one day be called Mesopotamia lay between two rivers. The rivers were the Tigris and the Euphrates. Sometimes the rivers flooded and washed rich bottom-soil up on the land. This made the land good for farming. People settled on this rich land. They grew their crops and raised animals. In the south, in a land called Sumer, another great civilization grew.

The people of Sumer are called Sumerians. Although the land they settled was fertile, it was not a perfect place to live. The weather was very hot in the summer. In spring there was always the danger of the rivers flooding. Sometimes whole villages would be washed away. Many people would die.

Part of Sumer was **swamp** land. Other parts were very dry. Land that was flooded in the spring dried hard under the late summer sun. It was necessary to make the land ready for crops. The Sumerian farmers had to get water from the rivers to their fields.

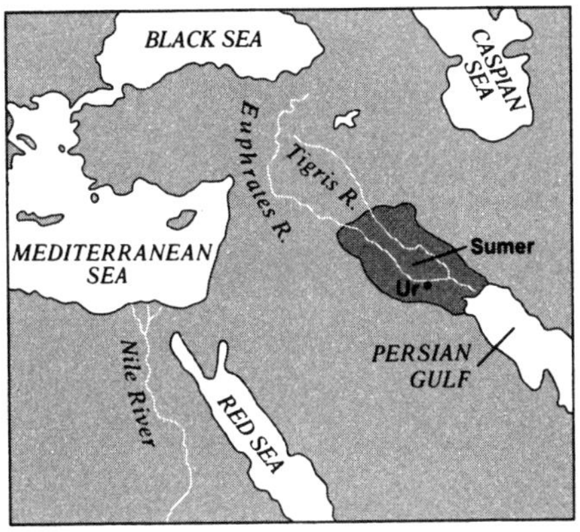

Sumer

Sumerian Farmers

The farmers found a way to **irrigate** their fields. They made cuts in the river banks and dug **canals**. The canals carried the river water out to the crops. The Sumerians also built **dikes** to hold back the flood waters.

A Sumerian farmer worked hard from early morning until late at night. His oxen were his treasure. They pulled the farmer's plow and carried the crops in from the field.

Sumer was a wealthy land, and its wealth lay in farming.

Trading

The people of Sumer had different jobs. While some were farmers, others were **merchants**. Sumer had no metal, stone, or timber of its own. Sumerians depended on trading to get these things. They sent their fine crops to other lands. In return, they brought back the goods that they needed at home.

Boats carried the goods to and from Sumer. The Sumerian boats were among the first ever used. There were two kinds of boats. River boats were small. They moved along under the power of long oars or poles. Trading ships were much longer, and they were narrow. They had big sails. The trading boats brought home treasures of gold, silver, pearls, and copper from other lands.

A Sumerian trading ship

A Sumerian river boat

Villages Grow into City-States

Ur-Namme, King of Ur, ca. 2300 B.C.

The earliest Sumerians lived in houses made from reeds. The reeds, or tall grasses, grew in the swamps. Later, the people learned to make bricks from mud. They dried the bricks in the sun and built houses from them. The brick houses stayed cool inside during the hot summers.

Each Sumerian village was built around a **temple**. The people believed a god or goddess lived in the temple and protected the village. The farmers took part of their crops to the temple to offer to the god. The priests of the temple became very wealthy and powerful.

Over the years, the villages grew. They became **city-states**, each one with its own government. A temple still stood at the center of each city-state. There was farmland all around the edge of the city. The city-states often fought among themselves. So the Sumerians built walls around their cities.

One of the great city-states of Sumer was called Ur. A gigantic temple called a **ziggurat** was built in Ur. This tall temple-tower was built to honor the god who watched over the city. The people of Ur came in great numbers to bring gifts to the temple. They believed that if their god was happy, the city would be wealthy.

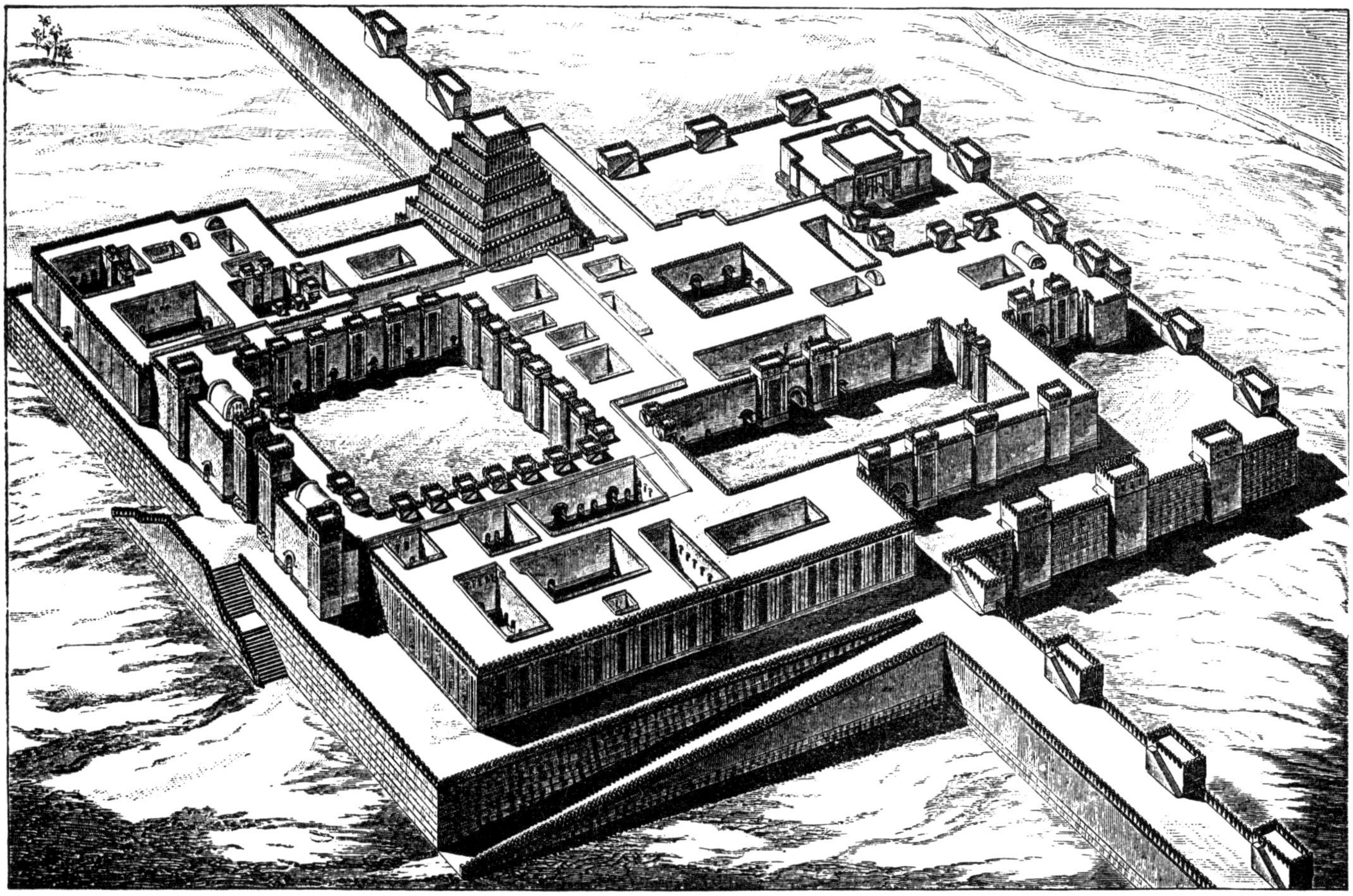

Ziggurat (tall tower near top)

The Invention of Writing

The Sumerians' inventions were their gifts to the world. All the civilizations that followed used inventions of the Sumerians. There are still things in the world today that date back to Sumer.

The greatest gift the Sumerians gave to the world was the invention of writing. The Sumerians were a wealthy people. So they needed some way to keep track of what they owned. They began by drawing pictures. They used a reed as a pen. They drew on soft pieces of clay. The soft clay was then dried in the sun. And the **tablet** became a permanent record.

Later, the Sumerian drawings changed. They began to look less like the real objects they represented. Instead, they became simple symbols that were easier to draw. Because of the shape of the reed, the symbols were wedge-shaped. This kind of writing is called **cuneiform.** By putting symbols together, the Sumerians could write whole sentences.

Ox *Symbol for ox*

Not all Sumerians knew how to write. Specially trained people called **scribes** learned how to write. They drew up business **contracts** for the farmers and merchants. The scribes were paid very well for their special skill. They were among the richest of the Sumerians.

We know a great deal about this earliest of civilizations. This is because Sumerian scribes wrote down their ideas and kept records.

Other Gifts from the Sumerians

The Sumerian farmers had to pay a tax on their property. And so the Sumerians invented a way of measuring land. Fields were divided into even squares. Then the squares were counted up to decide how much tax a farmer owed. Since the Sumerians used silver as money, payments were made in silver. The value of the silver was measured by its weight.

The Sumerians also learned to measure time. The 60-second minute and the 60-minute hour come from the Sumerian way of counting time.

Historians believe that the wheel was first used in Sumer. Sumerian armies rode in wheeled **chariots.** There were no horses in all of Sumer. So wild donkeys were taught to pull the chariots.

Irrigation canals came to us from the Sumerian farmer. And sailboats came from the traders.

Although there was no metal in Sumer itself, the Sumerians traded for metal. They became skilled metalworkers. They learned to make fine jewelry of copper, silver, and gold.

Sumerian ideas and Sumerian inventions brought about changes that would affect life for ages to come.

Life in Sumer

A Sumerian boy might awaken to a hot, dry summer day in the city of Ur. If his father were a farmer, the boy would go with him to work in the fields. They would leave their small house with the earliest rays of the sun. Perhaps that day the father and son would clean the irrigation canals. Even if the day were very hot, the boy would work hard. Those canals were important to the farm. Without them, nothing would grow. The boy might work alongside other farmers. They would have help from the slaves from one of the larger farms.

If the boy happened to be the son of a scribe or of a merchant, his day would be different. He might live in a bigger house, two stories tall. Boys from the wealthier families of Ur could go to school. School was a place for boys only. And a Sumerian school was not a place for fun! The boys sat from sunup until sundown on long benches. Baskets at their feet held reed pens and wet clay for tablets. The teachers made sure the boys worked hard. They learned to read, write, and do arithmetic. School rules were strict. Students were beaten when they did not learn their lessons.

Sumerian mosaic

But, if a boy learned well, he might become a scribe. A scribe could work in the king's palace or in the great temple itself.

The king ran the city of Ur. He ruled in the name of the city's god. Priests, scribes, and nobles helped him rule. These people were very rich. They lived a fine life. They were members of the highest classes in the Sumerian culture.

The people of Ur believed that when they died, they went to another world. Archeologists have discovered graves filled with fine gold jewelry. Some graves of the noblemen hold many skeletons. It may be that other people killed themselves, or were killed, when the noblemen died. This way they could follow the dead noblemen to that other world.

Attack on Ur

The Sumerian city-states fought with each other. So after a while Sumer grew weak. Around 2000 B.C. Sumerian cities came under attack. The Sumerian armies, even with their wheeled chariots, were not strong enough to save Sumer. Ur was destroyed. The city's wealth was stolen. Men and women were killed. Children were taken as slaves.

Soon other Sumerian cities fell, too. The invaders, called the Babylonians, built new cities. Later, some of those cities died away, too. Dust and dirt covered them over. Today archeologists dig into great mounds that still stand in the Middle East. Under the mounds of dirt lay all that is left of these ancient civilizations.

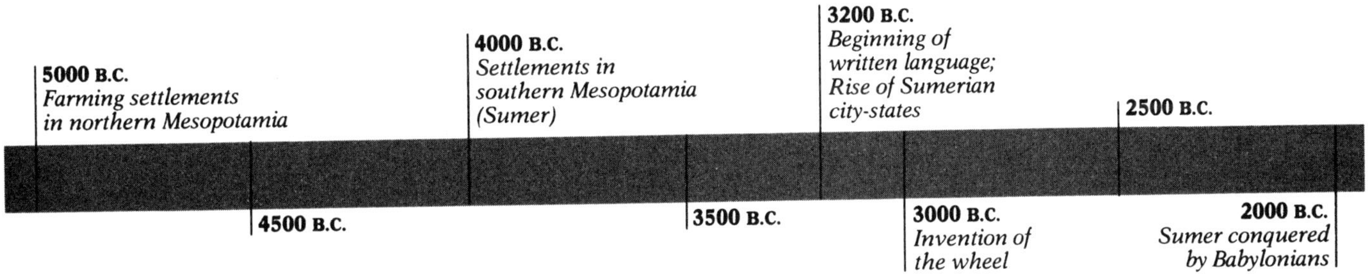

Points to Remember

- ◆ The first great civilization grew up between the Tigris and Euphrates rivers in the land of Sumer.
- ◆ The Sumerian civilization was based on farming.
- ◆ The Sumerians had to irrigate their land.
- ◆ The Sumerians traded with other lands for goods they needed.
- ◆ Sumerians lived in city-states. Each city-state had its own government.
- ◆ The Sumerians invented writing.
- ◆ The Sumerians invented the wheel, the sailboat, irrigation, and a way of measuring.
- ◆ The Sumerians were conquered, but their ideas lived on.

Think About It!

1. Name three Sumerian inventions.
2. The Sumerian civilization is a very old one. Give one reason why we know so much about it.
3. What did the Sumerians use as money?
4. How did the Sumerian civilization come to its end?

Chapter 4

Ancient Egypt: Land of the Pharaohs

Words to Know

desert dry, sandy land with little or no plant life

hieroglyphics a system of writing using pictures or symbols to represent objects, ideas, or sounds

mummy a dead body kept from rotting by being treated with chemicals and wrapped in cloth

papyrus a writing paper the Egyptians made from water plants of the same name

pharaoh a king of ancient Egypt

pyramid a huge stone structure with a square base and four triangular sides that meet in a point at the top. Egyptian rulers were buried in the pyramids.

tax money paid to support a government

tomb a grave, usually one that is enclosed in stone or cement

upstream in the direction against the flow of the river; at the upper part of a river

Look for the answers as you read:

1. Why did people settle along the Nile River?
2. What happened to the Nile River Valley every July?
3. Why did the powerful pharaohs have their people build pyramids?
4. What did archeologists find inside Egyptian tombs?
5. What were some Egyptian inventions?
6. How do archeologists think the pyramids were built?

The Pyramids, Egypt

Along the Nile

At one time the area now called the Sahara was a green plain. People lived there. There was water and wildlife. But the weather changed. The Sahara dried up and became a **desert**. The people living there went looking for water. Some of them went to a land called Egypt.

A great river called the Nile ran through Egypt. The Nile River Valley was a swampland. It was a dark jungle filled with dangerous animals. But the people needed water badly. So they cleared the land. They built their villages along the river where the jungle used to be.

Like the Sumerians, the people of Egypt built a civilization along a river. They were able to do this because the land along the Nile had what they needed. The Egyptians learned to farm, to tame animals, to make pottery, and to weave. They learned to make tools from metal.

Floods

The weather in Egypt was hot. But each year, in July, the Nile River spilled over its banks in a great flood. Land that stood dry all year was suddenly under water for several weeks. The floods left the land very fertile.

Farmers learned to use the floods to help them. They learned to save up some of the flood waters. Then they could water their crops during the rest of the year. Like the Sumerians, they learned to dig canals to irrigate their fields.

Each July the farmers moved to higher ground, taking their animals with them. They knew that the floods would be over in a few weeks. They waited until the Nile once again flowed peacefully within its banks. Then they planted their seeds in the rich, soft ground.

Lower Egypt and Upper Egypt Become One

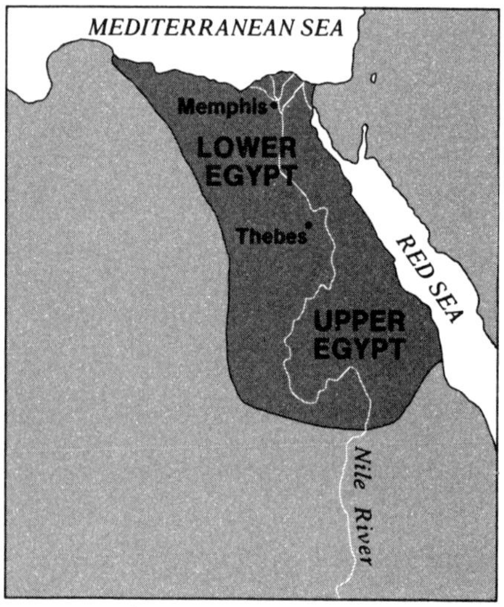

Upper and Lower Egypt

The civilization along the Nile did well. Villages joined together to form larger settlements. There came a time, around 3200 B.C., when two kings ruled all of Egypt. One king ruled Lower Egypt, in the north. Another king ruled Upper Egypt, in the south. A look at the map shows each of these areas. If a person in Lower Egypt followed the Nile River **upstream**, he would come to Upper Egypt.

The king of Lower Egypt wore a red crown. The king of Upper Egypt wore a white crown. The two kings ended up fighting to control all of Egypt. Around 3100 B.C. King Menes, of Upper Egypt, conquered Lower Egypt. Now Menes wore a "double" crown. He ruled all of Egypt.

The Pharaoh's Power

King Menes became the first great **pharaoh** of Egypt. The Egyptians called their rulers *pharaohs,* meaning *The Great House.*

The pharaohs were powerful rulers. Each year they collected **taxes**—huge taxes—from all the people. Farmers had to give the pharaoh a large part of their crops as a tax.

The pharaoh had many men to help him carry out his orders and collect the taxes. The pharaohs lived rich, splendid lives.

Ramses II, Egyptian pharaoh, reigned 1304–1237 B.C.

The Pyramids

The Egyptian pharaohs wanted people to remember just how rich and how powerful they were. Some had huge statues of themselves made. And they had their people build great **tombs** for them. When the pharoahs died, their bodies were placed in the tombs. Jewelry, food, clothing—all the pharaoh's favorite things—went into the tomb with him. The Egyptians believed that a person would need those things in the next world.

Egyptian wall painting

These great, towering Egyptian tombs are called **pyramids**. The pharaohs of Egypt, from about 2650 B.C. until 1637 B.C., were buried within those huge pyramids. There are many pyramids still standing in Egypt today. They are considered one of the wonders of the world.

The most famous pyramid is the Great Pyramid near Cairo. It covers an area larger than ten football fields. It contains more than two million stone blocks, each weighing about 2½ tons. Somehow, the stones had to be cut into shape and then transported to the building site. Then the stones were raised into place. They were laid so that they fit together exactly. From a distance the pyramid looks as if it were cut out of a single white stone. The Egyptians of 4,500 years ago had no machinery or iron tools. So how did they do it? We don't know for certain. In fact, we don't know if *we* would be able to build pyramids today, even with our modern building methods.

Building the Great Pyramid

The ancient Egyptians did use copper chisels. And they probably hauled the stones on some sort of wooden sled. Most likely they built a system of ramps and wooden planks to haul the stones into place. But mostly they had to rely on human muscle power. The ancient Greek historian Herodotus wrote about the pyramids. He said that 400,000 men worked each year for 20 years to build the Great Pyramid. Archeologists doubt these numbers. But we'll never know for sure.

Tombs within the pyramids have served as a wonderful record of the Egyptian civilization. Some tombs were broken into by robbers. And the artifacts were stolen. But archeologists have discovered some of the tombs. They were still filled with goods from daily Egyptian life. The walls of the tombs are covered with picture-writing. The pictures tell the story of the ancient Egyptian world.

Egyptian Mummies

Archeologists found more than bowls, pictures, jewelry, and pottery within the tombs. They found the pharaohs themselves! The Egyptians used certain chemicals to keep the dead body from rotting away. Of course, only the rich Egyptians could afford this special treatment.

Burying people this way was not a simple matter in ancient Egypt. First the brain and organs had to be removed from the body. Then the body was treated with a special chemical. It was then wrapped around and around in cloth bandages. A body wrapped like this is called a **mummy**. Many mummies were found deep within the Egyptian tombs. Egyptian mummies and artifacts have been taken from these tombs. They are on display today in museums around the world.

Egyptian mummy case

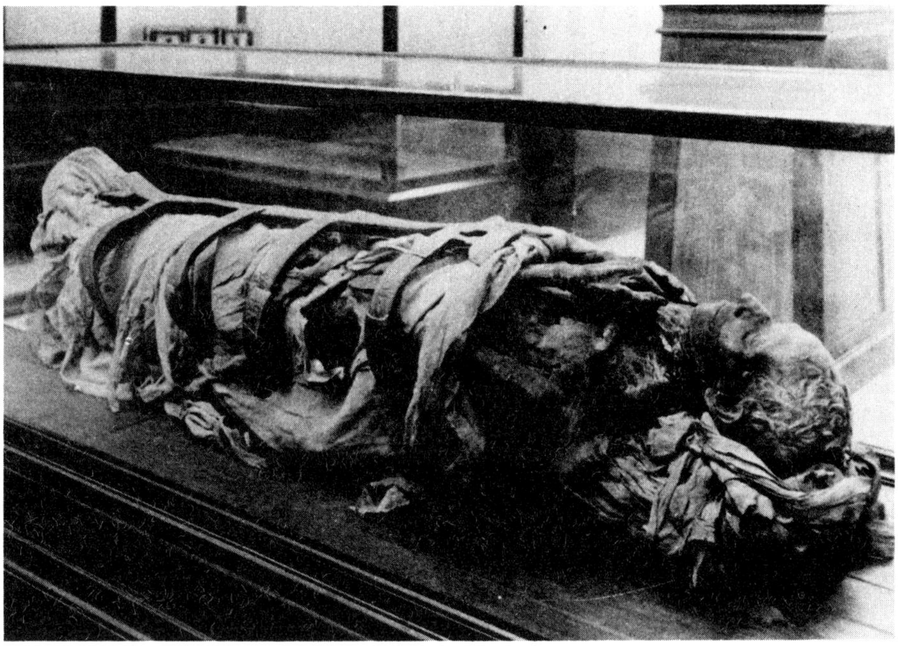

Egyptian mummy

Egyptian Gods

The ancient Egyptians believed in many gods. Just as in the land of Sumer, each city had its own special god. All Egyptians believed in Osiris, the powerful god of death.

The river played an important part in Egyptians' lives. It also played a part in their belief about death. They believed that the dead were ferried across a great river to meet Osiris in the next world.

Osiris, Egyptian god of the dead (center), with Isis and Anubis

Egyptian Beauties

The Egyptians were concerned about the way they looked. Drawings and statues show Egyptian women with long, dark hair worn in many braids and ringlets.

Both men and women wore makeup. They painted their lips red. They drew around their eyes with a dark green or gray paste called "kohl." And the Egyptians liked perfume. Both the men and the women rubbed sweet-smelling oils into their skins.

Husband and wife receiving offerings, wall painting

Egyptian Inventions

The Egyptian pharaohs and their nobles lived rich lives. But all the rest of the people led very simple lives. The farmers worked hard in their fields. There was usually plenty of food. So Egypt's craftsmen had more time to work on their skills.

Hieroglyphics carved in stone, Temple of Hathor, Abu Simbel, Egypt

The Egyptians learned to write. They invented a system of picture-writing called **hieroglyphics**. They learned to make paper from river reed, called **papyrus**. Our word *paper* comes from the word *papyrus.*

The Egyptians learned to chart the stars. And they decided that there were 365 days in a year.

The Egyptians made jewelry of gold and precious stones. They used metals for tools and weapons. The Egyptians made music, too. Archeologists have found ancient Egyptian instruments and the words to songs. The Egyptians built ships. They traded with other peoples.

The Sphinx, Egypt

But most of all the ancient Egyptians are remembered as the builders of the pyramids. The Egyptian builders have left us possibly the most amazing works of any civilization. And many of their secrets still lie buried within the pyramids.

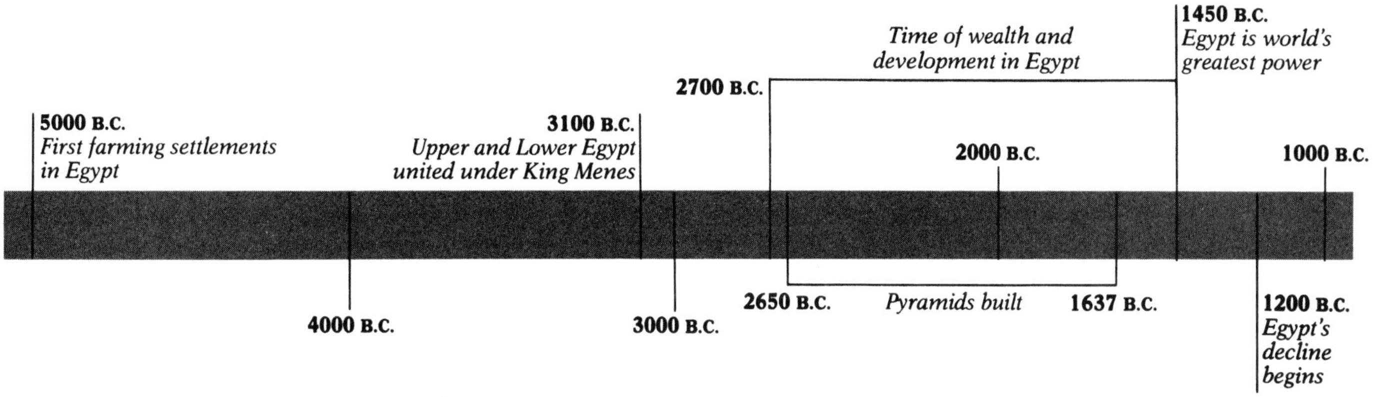

Points to Remember

- ♦ When the Sahara became a desert, people went to live along the Nile River.
- ♦ The river flooded each year, leaving the land around it fertile.
- ♦ Lower Egypt and Upper Egypt were united under King Menes.
- ♦ Egyptian rulers, called pharaohs, were very powerful.
- ♦ The pharaohs' tombs were in giant pyramids.
- ♦ Ancient Egyptians believed in life after death. And many of the things they owned were buried with them.
- ♦ We know a lot about the Egyptians from the artifacts found in their tombs.
- ♦ The Egyptians made paper from a reed called papyrus.

Think About It!

1. How did the yearly floods help the people who settled along the Nile River?
2. What kind of rulers were the Egyptian pharaohs?
3. Why did the Egyptians bury things from daily life along with a dead person?
4. Why are the pyramids called "wonders of the world"?

Chapter 5

Mediterranean Kingdoms

Words to Know

capital a city or town where the government of a nation or state is located

colonies groups of people who settle in a far-off land but are still under the rule of the land they came from

commandment a law or order, most often a religious law, as in the Ten Commandments in the Bible

conquer to get control by using force, as in a war

empire a group of lands all ruled by the same government or ruler

navigate to plan the course of a ship; to sail or steer

nomads people who move from place to place looking for food for their animal herds

siege the surrounding of a city by soldiers who are trying to capture it so that food, water, and other supplies cannot get in or out

treaty an agreement, usually having to do with peace or trade

tribe a group of people living together under a leader

tribute a payment or gift demanded by rulers of ancient kingdoms

Look for the answers as you read:

1. Where did the Phoenicians sail and trade?
2. For what two things did the Phoenicians become famous?
3. What religious belief made the Hebrews different from other Mediterranean people?
4. What religion grew out of the Hebrew civilization?
5. What was so special about the ancient city of Babylon?
6. Who was Hammurabi, and what was he known for?
7. What secret gave the Hittite army great military strength?
8. What did the Assyrians do when they captured a city?

Many groups of people settled along the eastern shore of the Mediterranean sea. Others settled the lands farther east. They farmed the fertile valley between the Tigris and Euphrates rivers. New civilizations began to grow. These groups traded with each other. They also made war with each other. They fought for control over the Mediterranean lands. Strong kingdoms took over smaller city-states. Powerful kings ruled **empires**.

One of these civilizations was the Hittites. They learned how to make tools and weapons out of iron. Other Mediterranean civilizations left their mark on world history in other ways. The Hebrews gave us the Jewish religion. And the Phoenicians invented an alphabet. It was very similar to our modern alphabet.

The Phoenicians: Traders on the Seas

The Phoenician civilization grew up along the eastern shores of the Mediterranean. It was unlike most of the other Mediterranean civilizations. The Phoenicians were not farmers. They built their cities on rocky shores. The Phoenicians were people of the sea. They were sailors and traders.

Few farm crops grew in Phoenicia. But there were plenty of trees. The people cut down the trees to use as wood for sailing ships.

The Phoenicians were the best sailors in the ancient world. They learned to use the stars to **navigate**. This made it possible for them to sail beyond the sight of land. The Phoenicians sailed where no other people dared to go. Their ships went to every corner of the Mediterranean. They reached the coast of Spain. They may even have sailed out into the Atlantic Ocean, beyond Gibraltar. They sailed along the west coast of Africa. Then they went all the way around the whole continent of Africa!

Phoenician explorers

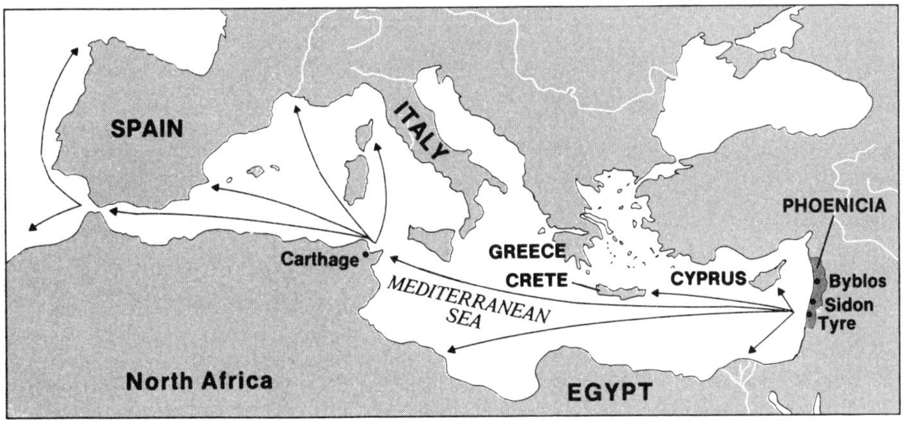

Phoenician trading routes

Wherever they traveled, the Phoenicians set up **colonies**. Their people settled in places all around the Mediterranean Sea. The Phoenician colonies became trading centers. One of the largest Phoenician colonies was Carthage. It was on the north coast of Africa. The people of Carthage traded their African gold, ivory, and ebony for Phoenician pottery, glass, and beads.

The colonies paid taxes to the Phoenician homeland. Great Phoenician cities, like Tyre, Sidon, and Byblos, grew rich and strong.

The Phoenicians were traders and sailors, not warriors. They paid soldiers from other lands to protect their cities. They built high, stone walls to protect themselves from attack.

Phoenician Inventions

The Phoenician ships were powered by oars and sails. They sailed all about the ancient world. And as the Phoenicians traded goods, they also traded ideas.

One of the most important ideas the Phoenicians spread was the alphabet. They turned pictures into letters. In fact, our own alphabet comes from the letters the Phoenicians invented.

Some Phoenician letters

Which letters look like those in our alphabet?

The Phoenicians became famous for another invention, too. It was a secret dye used to color cloth. The dye was made from snails that lived along the coast. The Phoenicians boiled thousands of snails to make just a tiny bit of dye. The dye was very costly. Named after the city of Tyre, it was called "Tyrian purple."

The Phoenicians traded the purple cloth. Only very rich people could buy it. Royalty throughout the Mediterranean world decorated their palaces with the purple cloth. They wore robes of Tyrian purple. The color purple came to stand for power and wealth. It became a royal color.

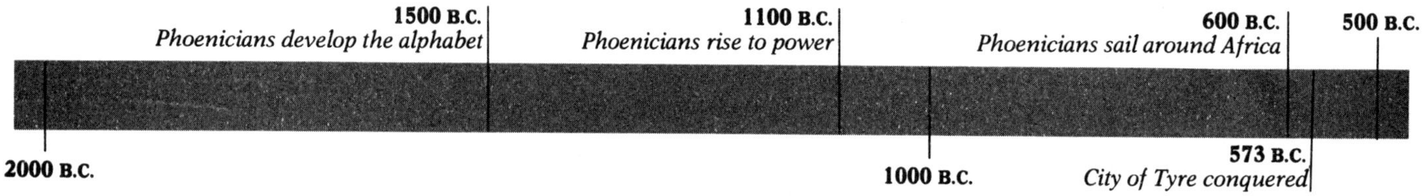

The Hebrews: Under One God

The Hebrews lived along the east coast of the Mediterranean Sea. Their civilization grew up just south of Phoenicia.

The Hebrews wanted their own land. They wanted a place where they could worship their god. In the Mediterranean world most people believed in many gods. There were gods of death and gods of the sun and rain. But the Hebrews believed in only one god.

The Bible says that a man named Abraham was the father of the Hebrew people. Abraham lived near the Sumerian city of Ur. One day he left with his family, to become a **nomad**. Abraham and his people followed their herds into a land called Canaan. When they found themselves short of food, they went on to Egypt.

Abraham's people, the Hebrews, were treated as slaves in Egypt. The Egyptian pharaoh was cruel. A man named Moses became the Hebrews' leader. He led them out of Egypt. He led them into the desert, away from the cruel pharaoh.

The Ten Commandments

The Hebrews did not find their land of freedom right away. They wandered, searching, for many years. The Bible says that during that time, Moses was given the Ten **Commandments**. It says that the commandments came directly from God. The commandments are laws to live by. They became laws for the Hebrews' religion, Judaism. The first commandment says that people must believe in only one god. "The Lord is One," the Bible reads. The Jewish religion was the first religion to teach belief in one God.

The Ten Commandments also tell how people should act toward each other. It is wrong to steal, the commandments say. It is wrong to kill. The Hebrews were the first to look upon hurting others as a sin.

Moses bringing the Ten Commandments

The Promised Land

David and Goliath

The Hebrews finally reached Canaan. They called it the "Promised Land." They believed it was the land that God had promised them. They settled there. They built towns. They followed their religion.

Holding onto the Promised Land was not always easy. A warlike people, the Philistines, lived nearby. The Philistines fought the Hebrews for their land.

There were 12 **tribes** of Hebrews. At first, the Philistines were able to **conquer** some of the tribes. Divided, the Hebrews were weak. But then, the tribes joined together under one king to fight the Philistines.

There is a famous story of a Hebrew shepherd boy named David. He fought a Philistine giant. The giant was called Goliath. David killed Goliath with a rock from a slingshot. The Hebrews then won the war against the more powerful Philistines.

David later became king of the Hebrews. The town of Jerusalem became his **capital** city. Jerusalem was a religious center and a trading center.

When David died, his son, Solomon, became king. Solomon built a beautiful temple in Jerusalem. He built a fleet of fine sailing ships. King Solomon was known to be good and to be very, very wise. Under his rule, Jerusalem became a mighty city.

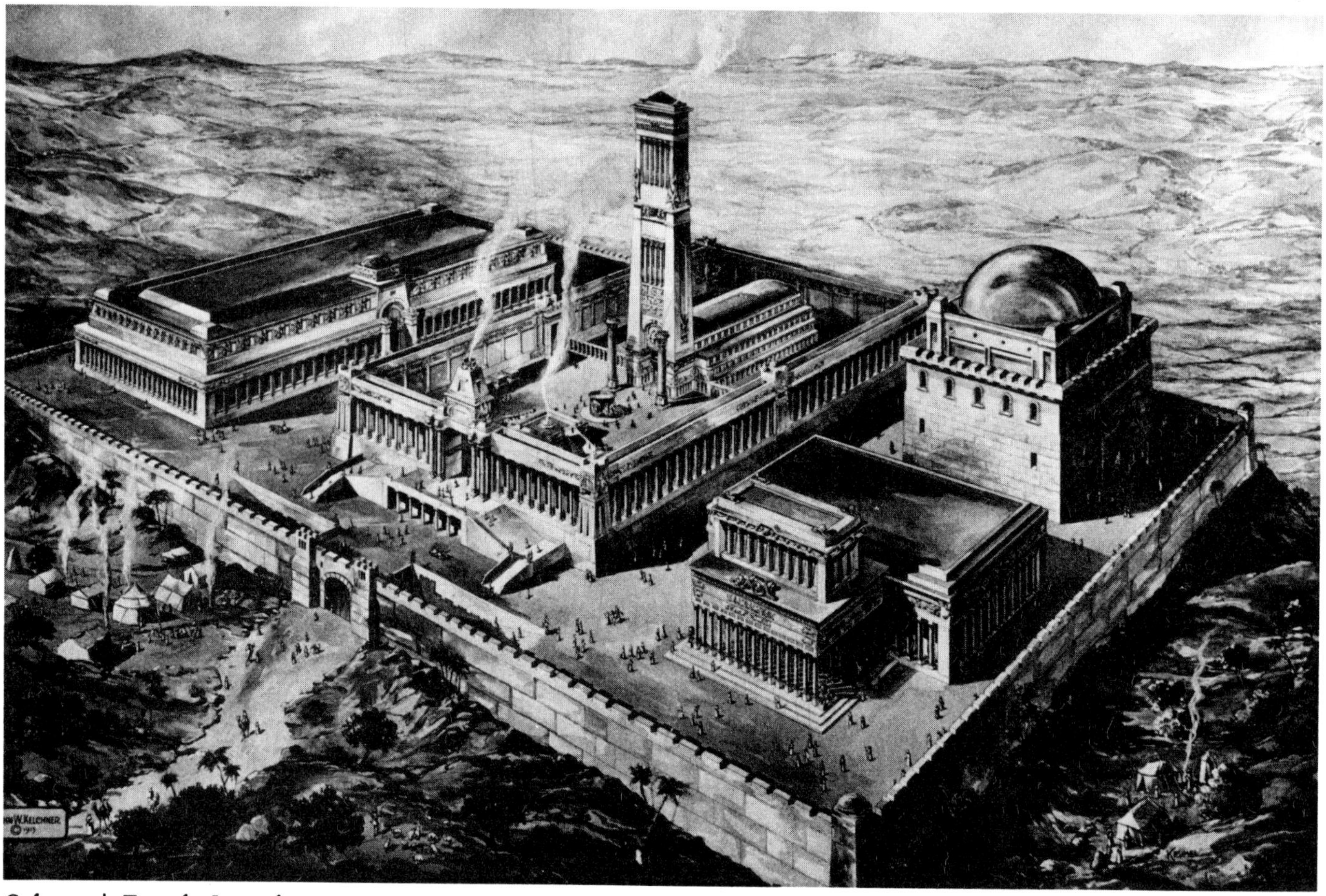

Solomon's Temple, Jerusalem

Israel and Judah

When King Solomon died, the Hebrew kingdom split. The tribes in the north made their own kingdom. They called it Israel. The people of Israel were the Israelites.

The tribes in the south formed the kingdom of Judah. Jerusalem was in Judah. The name of the Jewish religion came from the word Judah. And the people were called Jews.

The two kingdoms were in danger! For the next 200 years they fought. They fought each other. And they fought the powerful kingdoms that were all around them. These were the Egyptians, the Hittites, the Assyrians, the Babylonians, and the Persians. They all wanted control of the lands around Jerusalem.

At last the fierce neighbors were too strong. In 722 B.C. the Assyrians took over Israel. The Israelites were moved out or taken as slaves. About 150 years later, Judah fell to a Babylonian people known as Chaldeans. The Babylonian king destroyed Solomon's fine temple in Jerusalem.

And so it went. One power after another fought for the city that everyone wanted to control. Jerusalem was right in the middle of things. It came under many different rules. Today it is more than 2,500 years since the Babylonians destroyed the temple. Very little has changed. Different groups of people are still arguing over who should control Jerusalem.

Israel and Judah

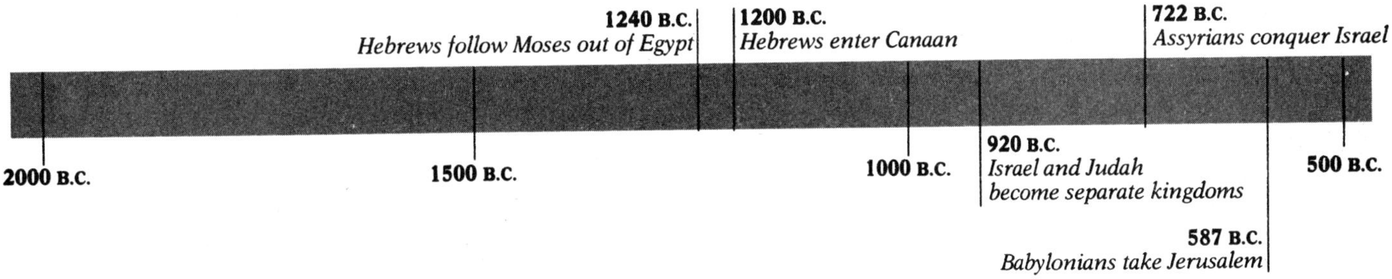

The Babylonians: The Rule of Law

Babylon was the capital city of the Babylonians. It stood on the banks of the Euphrates River. Little remains of it today. There are a few ruins in the middle of some dirt mounds. Archeologists have been digging through the ruins. They have learned that Babylon was one of the greatest cities of the ancient world. It contained some of the most beautiful temples and palaces to be found anywhere. The city was surrounded by big walls. They were decorated with blue glazed bricks and pictures of mythical beasts. People entered and left the city through huge bronze gates. Near the center of the city stood the great Tower of Babel. This tower is mentioned in the Bible. Not far from the tower were the Hanging Gardens of Babylon. The gardens were one of the wonders of the ancient world.

Babylon

Babylonia

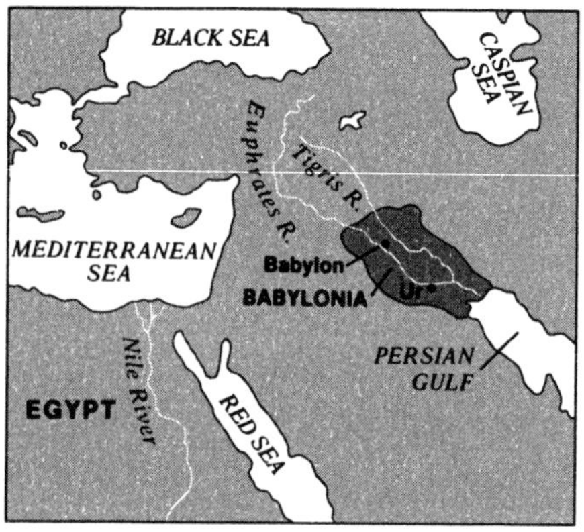

Babylon became an important city about 2000 B.C. This was nearly the same time that the Babylonians were destroying the Sumerian civilization. The Babylonians went on to build a large empire in what had been the land of the Sumerians.

The Code of Hammurabi

Hammurabi was one of the greatest kings of Babylonia. He ruled from about 1792 B.C. to 1750 B.C. Hammurabi created a system of laws. It was called the Code of Hammurabi. For the first time anywhere, there were laws to deal with almost every aspect of life. There were nearly 300 laws. They dealt with marriage and divorce, property and business, taxes, wages, loans, military service, and so forth. The Code also listed punishments for anyone who broke a law. People no longer had to depend on an "eye for an eye" when seeking justice. The Code was created to protect the rights of the individual citizen.

In time, the Babylonians were conquered by another people, the Assyrians. But some of the Babylonians' ideas about laws and justice have come down through the ages. They are included in our own laws today.

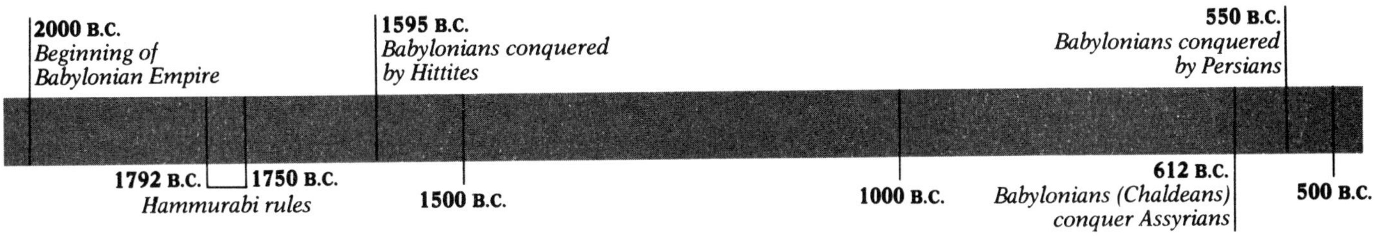

The Hittites and the Assyrians: Warrior Kingdoms

The Hittites and Assyrians were warriors. The Hittites came to the eastern Mediterranean around 2000 B.C. No one knows for sure where they came from. But they quickly swept through the lands called Anatolia. They found city-states already there. They conquered one after another. By 1650 B.C. the Hittites ruled all of these lands. Today this area is called Turkey.

The Hittites were mighty fighters. They used their might to create an empire. After they conquered Anatolia, they began attacking neighboring lands.

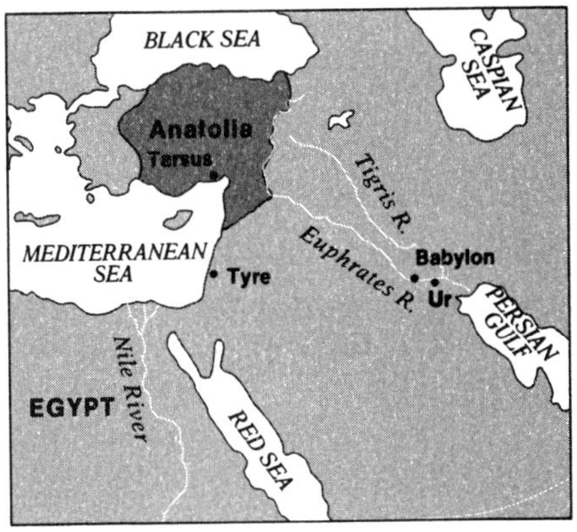

The Hittite Empire

The Secret

The Hittites had a secret that gave them their great power. For hundreds of years, they were the only people who knew how to make iron. Iron was strong. It made better weapons. No other people could beat the Hittite warriors and their iron spears.

The Egyptians looked upon the Hittites with great respect. They thought of the Hittites as the only other great power around the Mediterranean. In 1283 B.C., after years of fighting with each other, the Hittites and the Egyptians made peace. To help keep the peace, a Hittite princess married an Egyptian pharaoh.

The Hittites and the Egyptians signed an agreement to keep the peace. It became the first recorded peace **treaty**.

In time other people learned the secret of making iron. The Hittites were no longer the strongest. Around 1200 B.C. new people came and attacked the Hittites. They were called the Sea People. They came from islands in the Mediterranean. They brought about the end of the Hittite empire.

Hittite warrior

The Assyrians

The Assyrians were another warrior civilization. At first Assyria was a small kingdom. But when the Hittite civilization ended, the Assyrians began to look toward an empire of their own.

The Assyrians built up a great army. It was the best trained army of the ancient world. The Assyrians sent their army to attack the neighboring kingdoms. As more and more cities were captured, the Assyrian empire grew.

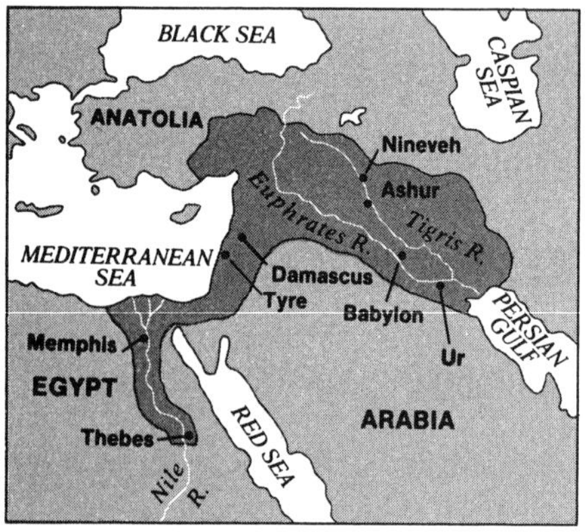

The Assyrian Empire

The Assyrians built their capital city on the banks of the Tigris River. The city was named Ashur, after one of the Assyrians' many fierce gods.

Assyrian kings were hard rulers. They made their people pay heavy taxes. Assyrians lived under strict laws. Anyone who broke a law could be cruelly punished. Many law breakers were beaten. Some even had their ears cut off!

Assyrian king

The Assyrian Army

The Assyrian civilization was a military one. All Assyrian boys knew what their future held. All men had to go into the army. The Assyrians needed soldiers in order to keep their power. And the Assyrians were builders as well as fighters. They built military equipment to help them conquer cities. They beat down city walls and gates with their huge machines called **siege** engines. A city under siege from fierce Assyrians stood little chance.

Assyrian warriors in battle

The Assyrians were not kind to the cities that they took. Sometimes they burned the city and killed the people who lived there. Often they took the people as slaves.

Sometimes, after they took over a city, the Assyrians acted as its new rulers. The people from the city had to pay **tribute** to the Assyrian king. If they did not pay the high price, they were punished.

Assyrian Developments

The Assyrian civilization did leave some things behind besides a successful military record. They built fine buildings and statues. They invented siege machines. But they also built machines to help lift water from the river into canals.

The Assyrians were among the first people to have a library. The library stored clay tablets with writings from the ancient world.

Even the fierce Assyrians were defeated at last. By 670 B.C. the empire was so big that it was hard to control. It began to break up. In 612 B.C. the Assyrian city of Nineveh was under siege itself. The Assyrian empire came to an end. The Assyrians had been conquered by a new Babylonian people—the Chaldeans.

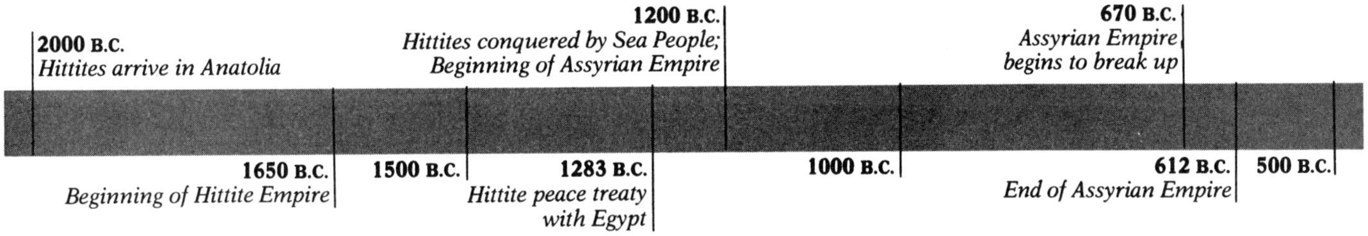

Points to Remember

- ◆ There were many kingdoms around the eastern Mediterranean Sea.
- ◆ The Phoenicians were sailors and traders.
- ◆ The Phoenicians developed an alphabet much like ours.
- ◆ The Hebrews started the Jewish religion and were the first to believe in one god.
- ◆ The Hebrews left slavery in Egypt to follow Moses to the Promised Land.
- ◆ The Hebrews lived by rules called the Ten Commandments.
- ◆ The Babylonian king Hammurabi created one of the earliest systems of laws.
- ◆ The Hittites and the Assyrians were both warlike civilizations.
- ◆ First the Hittites, and then the Assyrians, controlled the eastern Mediterranean world.

Think About It!

1. How did purple become known as a royal color?
2. How was the Hebrew religion different from others in the ancient world?
3. What happened to the Hebrew city of Jerusalem?
4. Why were the Babylonians lucky to have Hammurabi as a leader?
5. Why were the Hittites able to conquer cities and build an empire?
6. In what ways were the Assyrian kings cruel?

Chapter 6

Meanwhile . . . Around the World

Words to Know

ancestors people from whom one is descended

castes the social classes into which the people of India are divided

classes groupings of people according to social rank

dynasty series of rulers who belong to the same family

maize Indian corn

shrine a place of worship believed to be sacred or holy

Look for the answers as you read:

1. What was the "caste system" in India?
2. What people brought the caste system to early India?
3. What kept the Chinese empire separated from the rest of the world?
4. Why was it possible for large Chinese families to live together happily?
5. What very early Indian civilization developed in the Americas?
6. What new crops were grown in the Americas?

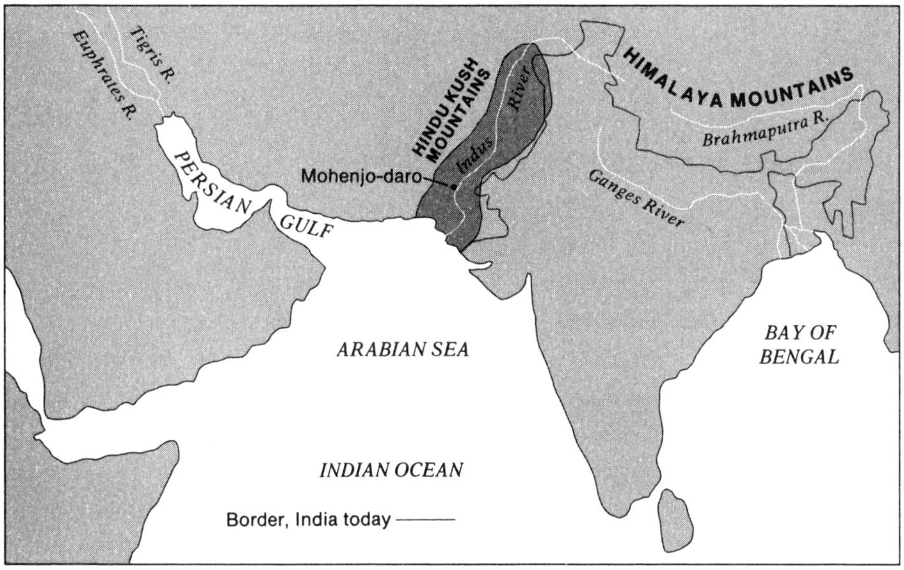

The Indus River Valley

Ancient India: The Indus River Valley

One of the world's earliest civilizations grew up around the Indus River. These lands are now known as India and Pakistan. The people, like so many others, settled near a river. They learned to irrigate their fields and to grow crops.

The people along the Indus made pottery, jewelry, and statues. They traded goods and ideas with the civilizations of the Fertile Crescent.

One of the main cities in the Indus River Valley was Mohenjo-daro. It was a fine, beautiful city. But it met a very sad end. Mohenjo-daro was a neat, well-planned city. It had long, straight main streets. Covered drainage systems ran under the streets. The people built brick houses. They even built apartment houses.

Life was good in Mohenjo-daro. The streets were clean. There were public swimming pools and bath houses. People could cool off on hot Indus Valley days. Brick courtyards circled shaded wells so that people and animals could drink in comfort. Many houses in Mohenjo-daro had their own indoor wells and tile-lined baths. Wheat and date palms grew on farms outside the city.

Mohenjo-daro stood peacefully for close to 1,000 years. Then, around 1500 B.C., the city was attacked. People from the north, the Aryans, swooped down on Mohenjo-daro. The Aryans showed no mercy. They ran through the steets of Mohenjo-daro killing most of the people.

Street in Mohenjo-daro

The Aryans believed that they were born to conquer and control. The word "Aryan" meant "nobleman" or "owner of land." The Aryans soon controlled all of the Indus River Valley.

The Aryans were fierce conquerors. But they also brought new ideas. They became known for making beautiful cloth decorated with gold and silver. And they also became known for their skilled doctors and mathematicians.

India's Caste System

The Aryans believed that they were better than the people they conquered. Their religion was based on the idea that some people are born "better" than others. Their religion developed into the Hindu religion. It divided all people into social **classes**, or **castes**. The Aryans divided people into four castes ranging from higher to lower:

1. priests and scholars
2. rulers and warriors
3. crafts workers, merchants, and farmers
4. unskilled workers

The Aryans called the people they conquered "outcastes" or "untouchables." The outcastes had no place in society. Any Aryan who married one of the conquered people would also become an outcaste.

Caste laws were strict. A person born into a certain caste would always stay there. No one could ever in his or her life rise to a higher caste. If somebody were very, very good, that person would be born into a higher caste in his or her "next life." If a Hindu led a bad life, he or she could be born again as an outcaste.

Rajas

The Aryans conquered the Indus Valley first. Then some of their tribes moved on to the east and to the south. They conquered one kingdom after another. The people who had been living there were forced to flee farther south. The Aryan tribes settled down in the lands that they conquered. They formed a number of city-states. Each one was ruled by a "raja" or prince. The rajas lived in fine palaces. Each raja had a highly trained army to protect his lands.

China: The Yellow River Valley

They called themselves the "Black-haired People." They lived in the valley of the Huang Ho, or Yellow River, in China. Their civilization grew up apart from the rest of the world. Steep mountains, wide deserts, and deep seas circled their lands. Northern China and the people of the Yellow River Valley were cut off from other civilizations.

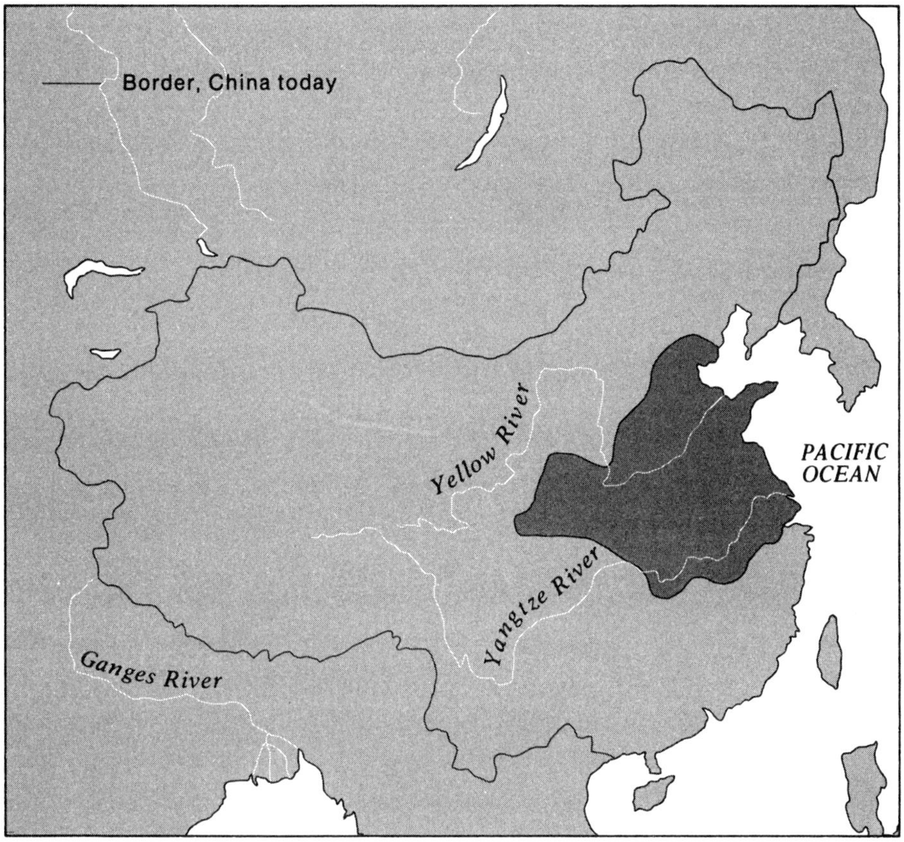

The Shang dynasty, Yellow River Valley, China

Most of the people in the Yellow River Valley were farmers. They fought floods that were so terrible the Yellow River became known as "China's Sorrow."

They dug pitlike houses in the ground and wove roofs of grass. Their kings lived in palaces made of wood and mud.

These early Chinese learned to write. They cut letters, or characters, into animal bones. They kept a record of their own history. It is one of the world's oldest written histories.

The people of the Yellow River Valley made fine cloth. They raised silkworms. They carefully unwound the long, thin threads that the silkworms spun. They wove the threads into silk cloth.

The Chinese had a special feeling for their **ancestors**. They also showed honor toward their homes, their families, and their land. There were many rules of courtesy in the Chinese culture. Those rules made it possible for large families to live together happily.

The Chinese culture did not change for many thousands of years. This is because people honored the ways of their ancestors. Also, the land was cut off from the rest of the world.

Chinese characters carved on bone

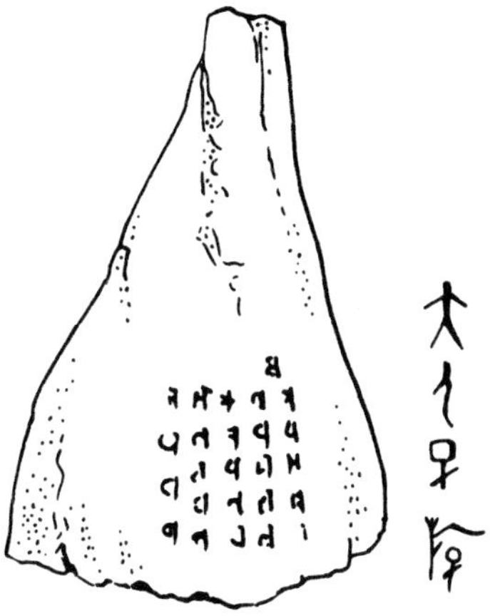

Chinese Dynasties

A period of rule in China is called a **dynasty**. For about 500 years "Shang" kings ruled the Yellow River Valley. This period is called the Shang dynasty.

Around 1028 B.C. a more warlike people, the "Chou," came to power. The Chou leaders developed systems of irrigation and flood control. And they extended their rule southward. Chinese civilization now reached from the Yellow River to the Chang, or Yangtze River. The powerful Chou dynasty lasted for more than 750 years. Finally, in 257 B.C., a different group of people took power.

Ancient Chinese warrior

Possible route to the Americas

The Americas: Faraway Lands

There were faraway lands that the people of the Middle East knew nothing about. For the most part, these lands were wild, thick woods and deep jungles. They were lands that would one day be known as North and South America.

A few tribes of people lived scattered across the Americas. These people would later be called Indians. Many scientists believe that these tribes first came from Asia. They say that the tribes traveled across a bridge of land and ice at the Bering Strait. Such a land bridge would have stretched 56 miles between Asia and Alaska. No trace of a land bridge exists now.

Why would these people have crossed the land bridge? Perhaps they were following animal herds. Then, over thousands of years, they kept on traveling south. Some stayed in North America. Others continued on to Central and South America.

For a long time, the people hunted and fished for their food. Then farming settlements began to spring up. This took place about 5,000 years after the people of the Middle East and Asia began farming. The new lands produced new crops. Farmers grew **maize**, or Indian corn. They grew squash and tomatoes and beans.

South American farmers grew cotton as early as 3000 B.C. They raised herds of tall, woolly animals called llamas. They wove the llama wool into beautiful cloth.

Llamas

The Olmecs

A people called the Olmecs built what might have been the first real city in the Americas. Their city was in Mexico, just west of the Gulf of Mexico. Archeologists have discovered Olmec jade and pottery dating back to 1200 B.C.

The Olmecs carved giant stone heads out of rock. Some of their carvings are more than nine feet tall! The Olmecs also built **shrines**. They built the shrines atop high mounds of earth. The Olmecs did an amazing job. They worked without metal tools and had not invented the wheel.

The Olmecs left some inventions behind. They had a system of counting. And they came up with a simple calendar. The Olmec civilization lasted over 1,000 years.

Ancient Olmec carved head

The Mayas

Just as the Olmec civilization ended, the Mayas arose. The Mayan civilization began in Mexico and Central America. The Mayas cleared jungles and built towns. They built temples to the gods of rain and of earth.

The Mayas used what the Olmecs had learned. They studied the Olmec calendar. Then they watched the sun, the moon, and the stars. They made their own calendar. It showed many feast days set aside to honor their gods. The Mayas built a strong civilization. This was at a time when tribes of nomads wandered most of the land.

Mayan temple, Chichen Itza, Yucatan, Mexico

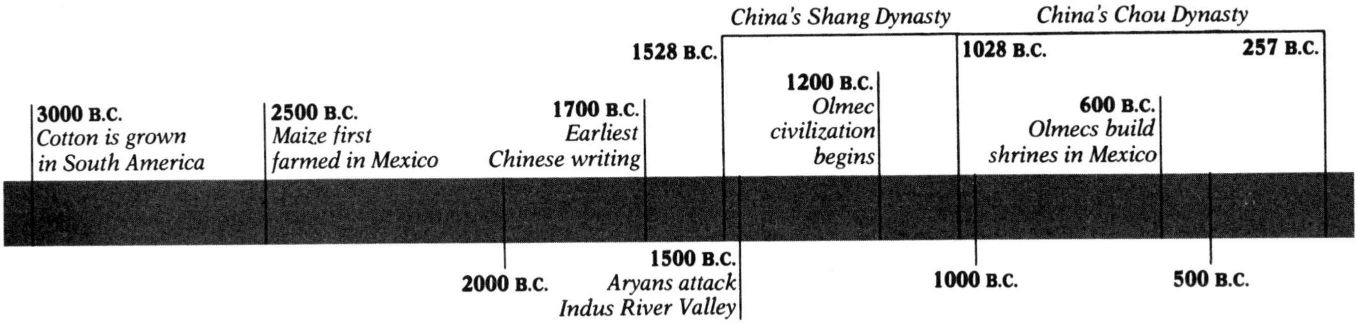

Points to Remember

- ♦ An early civilization developed along the Indus River in India.
- ♦ Aryans conquered the Indus Valley settlements.
- ♦ The Aryans brought a caste system that divided all people into social classes.
- ♦ An early Chinese civilization grew up along the Huang Ho, or Yellow River.
- ♦ Tribes of people probably crossed a land bridge from Asia to the North American continent. These tribes moved south and settled in Central and South America.
- ♦ The Olmecs were one of the earliest civilizations in the Americas.
- ♦ The Mayas were another highly developed early civilization in Mexico and Central America.

Think About It!

1. Could a person born in India to a family of farmers hope to go to school and become a scholar?
2. Why do you think so many civilizations grew up near rivers?
3. How do scientists think that people got from Asia to the Americas?
4. Think about all the different ancient civilizations you have studied. Were some of their inventions the same? Name some that were the same.

Chapter 7

Greece: The Golden Age

Words to Know

athlete a person trained to take part in competitive sports. The ancient Greek word *athlete* means "one who tries to win a prize in a contest."

citizen a person who has certain rights and duties because he or she lives in a particular city or town

constitution the laws and rules of a government

democracy a government that gives the people the ruling power

jury a group of people who listen to the facts and decide if a person on trial is guilty or not guilty

military having to do with soldiers or the armed forces

myths stories, often about gods or heroes, that are handed down through the years and sometimes used to explain natural events

plague a deadly disease that spreads quickly

revolt to rise up against a government; to refuse to obey the people in charge

tyrant a ruler who has complete power

Look for the answers as you read:

1. What are two different ways that Greek city-states were governed?
2. How was life in Sparta different from life in Athens?
3. What kind of government did Athens have?
4. Who won the Persian Wars?
5. Why is the time following the Persian Wars called the "Golden Age"?
6. What two city-states fought against each other in the Peloponnesian War?

The Greeks were people with ideas! Greek thinkers asked questions about everything. They wanted to learn as much about their world as they could.

Most early civilizations were mainly farming societies. But the Greek civilization was different. Greece is a very rocky land with many mountains. Much of Greece made poor farmland. The Greeks could not grow much wheat or other grains. Instead, they raised grapevines and olive trees. And Greece is surrounded by the sea on almost every side. So the Greeks took to the sea and became traders.

The Aegean Sea and the Mediterranean Sea made perfect travel lanes. The Greeks traded with most of the Mediterranean world. Greek traders set up colonies in the lands they visited. Greek culture spread across the seas.

Ancient Greece

Greek harbors were always busy. The air was filled with sounds. There was the clink of Greek coins and foreign coins. There was the chatter of many different languages as people of the world met. Merchants traded wheat for olive oil. Ships from Egypt unloaded papyrus. Ebony and ivory came in from Africa.

Greek City-States

The earliest people who settled in Greece began to build villages about 1500 B.C. As time passed, the small villages grew into city-states. Through trading, the city-states became wealthy. By about 750 B.C. the Greeks had begun to build colonies in other areas of the Mediterranean. Some Greeks settled on the Greek islands. But many others traveled as far as southern Italy, France, Spain, and Portugal. They built cities there. Naples, Syracuse, Marseille, and Lisbon began as Greek cities. Cities were also built in western Turkey and on the shores of the Black Sea.

On the Greek mainland, the city-states were becoming more powerful. The city-states were separated from each other by rugged mountain ranges. For this reason there was limited contact between the city-states. Each one developed in its own way.

Each city-state had its own government. And each had its own idea about the way people should live. Some of the city-states were ruled by a **tyrant**, a single powerful man. Some of the tyrants were cruel and unjust. But some of them ruled fairly. Other city-states let citizens vote and have a say in the government. This type of city-state was the earliest example of a **democracy**.

Because the city-states were so different from each other, they often fought among themselves. A tyrant with big ideas would decide that the time had come to expand his rule. He would make plans to attack a nearby city-state. He might convince other city-states to join him. There was a constantly shifting pattern of friendship and hostility between the different city-states. This was a very unstable political situation. It would later lead to a major war between two of the largest city-states, Athens and Sparta.

The Acropolis

Each city-state was made up of a city circled by villages and farms. The farms provided food for the citizens. The city offered protection from invaders.

The Greeks usually built their city-states near a high hill. The hill was called the Acropolis. On that hill, they built special buildings—temples, theaters, and banks.

The people who lived in Athens built a beautiful temple atop their Acropolis. It was built to honor the goddess Athena. The temple was called the Parthenon.

The Parthenon, Athens, Greece

Athens and Sparta

Athens and Sparta were the most powerful Greek city-states. Their citizens spoke the same language. They believed in the same gods. But life in Athens was very different from life in Sparta.

The Spartans lived in a **military** society. Sparta's government was led by a small group of men. They were most interested in keeping Sparta a great military power. Spartan children belonged to the state. A healthy boy was turned over to the government at the age of seven. He was raised to be a soldier. He was taught to fight and to stand up under pain. He had to obey orders without question. Soldiers defeated in battle were not allowed to return home.

Spartan warriors (on left)

If a baby boy were born with something wrong, he might be left on a hillside to die. The Spartans only wanted boys who could grow up to be soldiers. And Spartans had little use for girls. Girls and women were seldom seen in public. They kept to their houses. The Spartans were great warriors. But they left the world little in the way of ideas, or art, or music.

The Spartans, like most of the Mediterranean peoples, kept slaves. Most of the work in the city was done by slave labor. The Spartan army was often kept busy fighting other city-states. At other times it had the job of keeping rebel slaves in line.

Socrates

While life was harsh in Sparta, things were very different in Athens. The Athenians gave less thought to warfare. They were more interested in enjoying life.

Athens was a wealthy city. The Athenians decided that their wealth gave them more time to enjoy the beauties of life. They wanted their city to be glorious. They built the Parthenon. Their marble statues show the human body in its most ideal form. They put on plays in huge outdoor theaters. For the first time, plays were written about how people think and act. Some of these plays are still performed today.

The Athenians took time to ask questions about their world. Great teachers, like Socrates, led the Greeks to ask, "What makes people good? What makes people evil?" "Always ask questions," Socrates taught. So the Greeks questioned, and they learned.

A young student of Socrates, a writer named Plato, even questioned slavery. That slavery might be wrong was a brand new idea. Most of the ancient world had slaves as laborers. In Athens, too, work was done by slaves. But a few Athenian thinkers were possibly the first to ask, "Is it right for people to own other people? Is it right to force a person to labor for another?"

Democracy

In Athens' early years, government was in the hands of landowners. If a man owned land, he was a **citizen**. He had a voice in running the city-state. As the city grew, many merchants and business people, shippers and traders became wealthy. They did not own land, but they wanted a say in city government. They wanted to be citizens!

A **revolt** led to new government. In 508 B.C. this government drew up an Athenian **constitution**. Under the new laws, all free men were citizens. Only women and slaves did not have the rights of citizenship.

A citizen had the right to vote. And he was expected to hold office if called upon, sit on a **jury**, and serve in the army. The Athenian democracy was a government "by the people." It served as a model for our own democratic government. The main difference was that so many of "the people" (women and slaves) were not allowed to be citizens then.

Greek Religion

The Greeks believed that people were very important. They celebrated the human mind and the human body. Therefore their gods were much like humans. The Greeks worshiped many gods and goddesses. They gave each one a name and a humanlike form and personality. The gods and goddesses, according to the Greek storytellers, lived on top of Mount Olympus. This is the highest mountain in Greece. There, they enjoyed life. They laughed and they argued just as humans do. They played tricks on each other and on the humans they ruled.

The Greek god Zeus

Zeus was the king of the Greek gods. His wife was Hera, queen of the gods. The Parthenon on the Athenian Acropolis was built to honor Athena. She was the goddess of wisdom and learning.

The Greeks told **myths**, which are stories about their gods. The myths explained things in nature. They told of the doings of the gods and goddesses.

Myths were told about jealous gods and angry gods. And there were gods who fell in love with humans and gods who helped humans. Greek myths made exciting stories.

The Persian Wars

As Greek city-states grew strong and wealthy, another land began to look toward Greece. The Persian Empire under Cyrus the Great had become the strongest military power in the world. Around 550 B.C. Persia attacked and conquered the Greek colonies in Lydia. This was along the coast of what is now called Turkey. About 60 years later, the Greeks in Lydia tried to revolt. King Darius I of Persia crushed their uprising. Then he sent his huge army to invade Greece.

In 490 B.C. the Persian armies headed for Athens. On the plain of Marathon, the Athenians beat the mighty Persians! An excited Greek citizen ran 26 miles (40 kilometers) to Athens to spread the good news. An Olympic event of today is named after that run from Marathon to Athens.

But the Persians were not ready to give up. Darius's son, Xerxes, continued the war. About ten years later, Xerxes led an even stronger force into Greece. The Greek city-states put aside their quarrels in order to fight the common enemy. Xerxes's navy attacked. Spartans fought the Persian invaders long and hard. But the Persians were too strong. Xerxes's men attacked the city of Athens next. They destroyed the Parthenon and burned much of the beautiful city.

Xerxes left Athens thinking that he had won the war. But he was in for a surprise. His men met the Athenian navy off the harbor of Salamis. There was a great sea battle. The Persians were defeated. The Greeks sent the Persians back across the Aegean Sea. And Greece was left to enjoy a time of peace.

The Golden Age

The peace following the Persian Wars lasted for about 50 years. During that time, Athens grew in power and strength. It became the greatest city-state in Greece.

Athens collected money from the other city-states. The Athenians insisted that their navy must be kept strong in order to protect all of Greece.

A great Athenian leader named Pericles rose to power in 461 B.C. Pericles helped the Athenians continue their democratic government. He used some of the money collected from other city-states to rebuild the Parthenon.

Athens flowered with Pericles as its leader. It was a time known as the "Age of Pericles," or the "Golden Age of Athens." The Athenians, at peace now, had time to study science and geography. They wrote their greatest plays and created their finest statues.

Athens of the Golden Age was one of the most beautiful cities in the world. Many other Greek city-states followed the Athenians' way of life and their ideas of democracy.

But Sparta continued as a military state. The Spartans did not like the way Athens was building and growing. And they were angry that Athens had been collecting money from the rest of Greece.

The Peloponnesian War

Peace ended in 431 B.C., when Sparta led some of the other city-states against Athens. Sparta was a land power with a strong army. Athens was a sea power. Most of its strength was in its navy. Both cities fought for control of Greece. The war between Athens and Sparta was called the Peloponnesian War. It was named after the Peloponnesus, the part of Greece in which Sparta was located. This war went on for 27 years!

The Spartans tried to cut off supplies to Athens in order to starve the people. But the Athenians held on, even though the Spartans were among the world's best fighters.

Then a terrible **plague** broke out in the city of Athens. One-fourth of the Athenian people died during the plague. Their leader, Pericles, was among those who died.

Athens could no longer hold out against Sparta. In 404 B.C. Athens surrendered to Sparta.

Gifts from the Greeks

Greek thought and Greek works are very much a part of life today. Greek ideas in building show up in modern buildings. Greek statues still influence today's artists. The style of art and architecture the Greeks developed is called the "classical" style.

Today's students still read the works of Greek thinkers like Socrates, Plato, and Aristotle. "Know yourself," the great teachers said. "Ask questions. Search for the truth."

The Greeks were the first people to ask, "What is the world made of? Why is it the way it is?" They developed ideas about the sun, the earth, and the stars.

"The earth is round," Eratosthenes said. "The earth moves around the sun," Aristarchus said. Rules of geometry were invented by Greeks like Euclid and Pythagoras.

Classical Greek columns

We can also thank the Greeks for a model of a democracy. "Our government is called a democracy because power is in the hands of the whole people," said the Athenian leader, Pericles.

Greek words and ideas show up in our own language. *Astronomy, biology, geography,* and *geology* are all taken from the Greek language. So are the words *music, theater, drama, comedy,* and *tragedy.*

The word **athlete** comes from the Greeks, too. Our Olympic Games are athletic contests. They are modeled after those played by Greek athletes so long ago.

The first known Olympic games took place in 776 B.C. Early Olympic games were held to honor the gods. They were held every four years at the temple of Zeus in Olympia. All wars in Greece had to stop when it was time for the Olympic games. The athletes came from Athens and Sparta and all the other city-states.

The Discus Thrower

The earliest Olympic games were just foot races. Later the Greeks added boxing, wrestling, jumping, discus throwing, chariot racing, and other sporting events.

Today, just as in early Greece, it is a great honor to win an Olympic event. Winners get medals of gold and silver and bronze. In ancient Greece the winners were crowned with a circle of laurel leaves. The athletes brought glory to their city as well as to themselves.

The Greek leader Pericles saw the greatness of Greece in the Golden Age. He was proud of the wonders of his city, Athens.

"Mighty indeed are the marks and monuments of our empire . . . ," Pericles said. "Future ages will wonder at us. . . ."

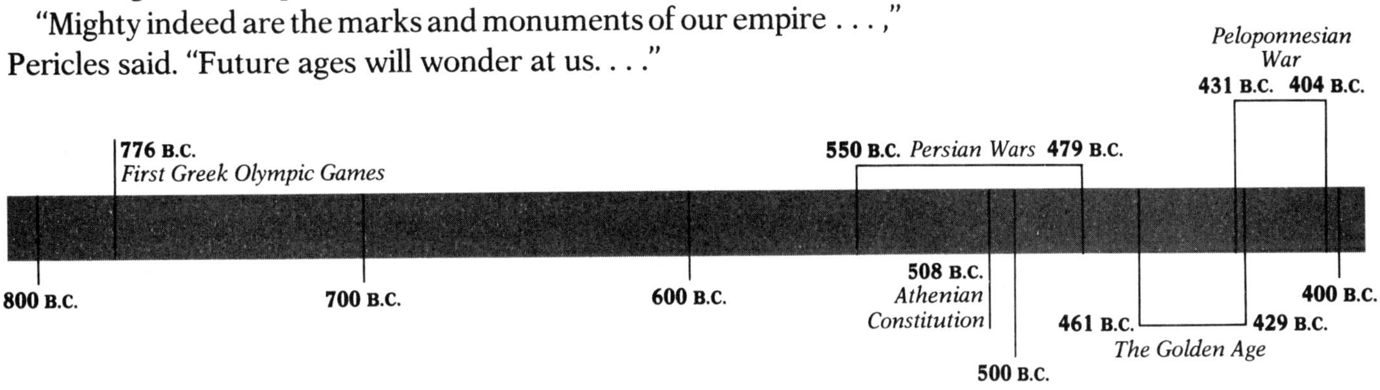

Points to Remember

- ◆ Most of Greece's wealth came from trading rather than from farming.
- ◆ Greece was divided into city-states, each one with its own government.
- ◆ Athens and Sparta were two powerful city-states.
- ◆ Athens was a democracy and would serve as a model for our own government.
- ◆ Sparta had a military government.
- ◆ The Greeks worshipped many humanlike gods.
- ◆ The Greeks fought the Persians, and they drove the Persian army away.
- ◆ Quarrels between Athens and Sparta turned into the Peloponnesian War. Sparta won.
- ◆ The Greeks were great thinkers. Because they questioned their world, they learned.

Think About It!

1. If you were a Greek of long ago, would you rather have lived in Sparta or in Athens? Why?
2. Which people could be citizens of Athens?
3. Name two Greek gods or goddesses.
4. Who led the Athenians during the "Golden Age"? Why do you think it was called the Golden Age?
5. Tell about something we do today that started in Ancient Greece.

Chapter 8

Alexander the Great

Words to Know

ambition the drive to become powerful, successful, or famous

assassinate to murder a leader or other important person

campaign a series of battles all aimed at one military end

conqueror a person who gains control by winning a war

generals high military officers

Look for the answers as you read:

1. Where was Macedonia?
2. How did King Philip II of Macedonia become ruler of Greece?
3. Who was King Philip's son?
4. Why was Alexander called the "Great Conqueror"?
5. Why did Alexander decide to make Babylon the capital of his empire?
6. What happened to Alexander's kingdom after his death?

King Philip of Macedonia

The Peloponnesian War was over. The Greek city-states were now under Sparta's rule. But they still argued with each other.

To the north was a land called Macedonia. It was ruled by a king named Philip II. Macedonia had always been poor. But things changed when Philip became king. Philip saw to it that Macedonians farmed their good soil. He sent out Macedonian traders. He built new roads. King Philip II had ideas.

Philip built up the Macedonian army. He built war machinery. He taught his men new ways of fighting. Philip soon had a strong army of foot soldiers and soldiers on horseback.

King Philip had an eye to the future. His plan was to conquer the great Persian Empire.

But to do that, Philip needed military strength. He needed more strength than he had with only Macedonia behind him. Philip wanted the power of all the Greek armies.

King Philip told some of the nearby city-states about his plan. They agreed to join him. But Philip needed more power. He needed the largest city-states, Athens and Thebes, behind him. So he used all his military know-how along with his well-trained men and their fine machinery. And Philip conquered Athens and Thebes.

Soon all of Greece fell under Macedonian control. All except Sparta, that is. Philip never conquered Sparta.

Now Philip was ready for war with the Persians. But King Philip II would never lead his men into Persia. By now he had made enemies. There was a plot to **assassinate** him. And before he could begin his **campaign** against Persia, he was killed.

Philip's Son

Philip had a son, Alexander. Alexander was not an ordinary boy. From his father, Alexander inherited **ambition** and a love of power. Philip taught his boy all about warfare and leadership. Alexander's mother, Olympias, was said to be very smart and very hot-tempered. Alexander, too, was bright and very easily angered.

As a boy, Alexander seemed almost fearless. Stories tell of the young Prince Alexander taming a certain horse. No other person in the kingdom could ride it. Alexander named that horse Bucephalus. Bucephalus would carry Alexander across an empire!

King Philip always thought highly of the Greek way of life and of Greek ideas. His son, Alexander, was to have the best of teachers—the Greek thinker, Aristotle. At age 14, Alexander began his lessons.

Alexander the Great

Aristotle taught Alexander to love Greek stories of heroes and adventure. He taught the boy about far-off lands and about other cultures. Aristotle saw to it that Alexander took part in sports, too. The young boy kept his body and his mind ready and strong.

By the time Alexander was 18, he was able to take a command in his father's army. Alexander was 20 when his father was killed. Now he was ready to take over as king of Macedonia. He was ready to become a **conqueror**.

Aristotle

Alexander, the Great Conqueror

Philip II had planned to conquer an empire. Greece would be the center of that empire. And Greek learning and culture would spread from there. Now that job fell to his son, Alexander.

Since birth, Alexander had been raised to be a ruler and a warrior. He was ready for the job. Alexander and the Macedonian army headed for Persia.

The next two years saw Alexander and his men crossing the Middle East. They conquered one land after another. Then in 334 B.C. Alexander began his campaign against Persia. In 333 B.C. Alexander did battle with the king of the Persian Empire, King Darius III. Alexander won the battle, but King Darius escaped.

On through the Persian Empire, on to Syria, swept the conquering Macedonians. They attacked the great Phoenician city of Tyre. Alexander ordered his men to build a raised road over the sea to reach the city. His battle at Tyre was one of his greatest military victories.

After taking over Phoenicia, Alexander moved south, toward Egypt. He was out to conquer the whole world!

Alexander in Egypt

Alexander had an easy time in Egypt. The Egyptians had been under harsh Persian rule. They were glad to see the conquering Macedonians. They accepted Alexander as their new ruler. Some Egyptians even hailed Alexander as the son of an Egyptian god. Alexander liked that idea!

Alexander built a city on the Mediterranean coast of Egypt. He named it after himself, like many other cities he had built. Egypt's *Alexandria* became the most famous of the Alexandrias.

It was a beautiful city. Many of its buildings were Greek in style. A giant lighthouse there rose 370 feet high. This lighthouse has been called one of the wonders of the ancient world. Alexandria had fine schools and a huge library. It became a center for scientists and inventors. The glory of Greece had come to Egypt.

One of Alexander's **generals** was named Ptolemy. Alexander left him to rule as Egypt's king. Ptolemy's family would rule Egypt for 300 years.

The End of the Persian Empire

Alexander was more interested in conquering than in ruling. Just as with Ptolemy in Egypt, he would set up many more kings to rule other lands. Alexander felt his work was done. He moved on from Egypt. He still wanted the whole world.

In 331 B.C. Alexander met King Darius III of Persia again. Alexander defeated Darius. And, once again, Darius escaped. But Alexander had no more trouble with his old enemy. King Darius was to die that same year, killed by his own men. With Darius gone, Alexander was the ruler of all the Persian Empire.

The city of Persepolis, in southwestern Persia, was the greatest city of the Persian Empire. Much of the wealth of the Empire was stored in the palaces of Persepolis. Alexander and his army easily captured the city. They killed most of the people who lived there. They took the rest as slaves. The Macedonians took all the treasures and then burned the Persian palaces. In 480 B.C. the Persians had burned Athens. Now Alexander had gotten even.

Then Alexander looked east. What was left for him in the world? India would be next.

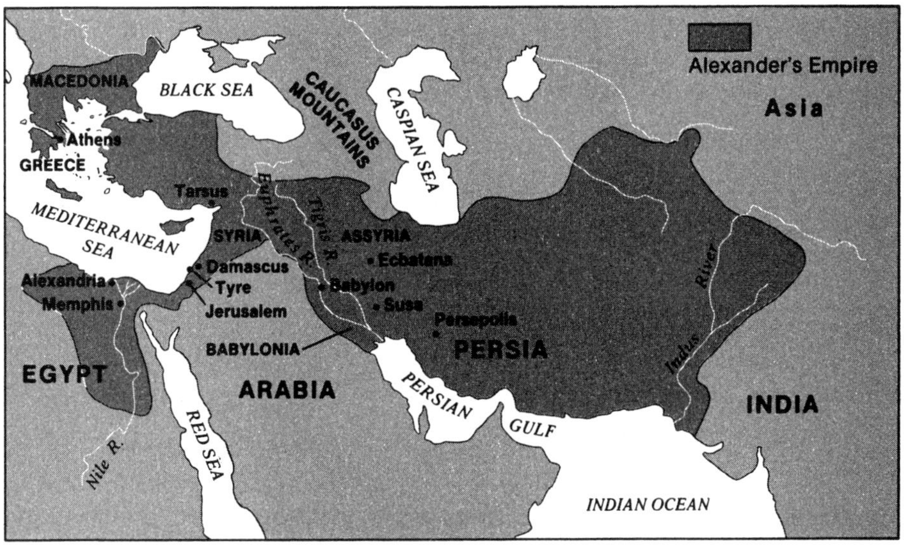

Alexander's Empire

Alexander in the Valley of the Indus

Alexander the Great arrived in India. The Aryan rajas along the Indus River battled the Macedonian soldiers. The Aryans rode great, lumbering war elephants. This was something Alexander had never seen before. But Alexander's men, riding horseback, were faster. Alexander conquered the Indus River Valley.

Alexander wanted to go on, deeper into India. He wanted more land, more kingdoms. But his men were tired. Heavy rains had come, and marching was hard. They wanted to go home.

"Back to Greece," they cried.

"On through India," Alexander demanded.

But his armies had been on the move for twelve years. They insisted on turning back. They would go no farther. And Alexander had to give up his campaign.

Alexander's Empire

Alexander was 30 years old when he conquered the Aryan kingdoms in India. He had been fighting and building his empire for twelve years. In all that time he had never lost a single battle!

Alexander made his father's dreams real. He spread Greek culture and ideas over a large part of the world. The lands Alexander touched would always show something of Greek style and Greek customs. Alexander's empire was the largest the ancient world had ever known.

Alexander imagined Europe and Asia as one big country, united under his rule. He wanted to blend the two into one. He chose Babylon as his capital city because it was in the center of his empire. He had plants brought in from one continent and planted on the other. Alexander married an Asian woman. And he rewarded his soldiers if they did the same.

Alexander ruled a giant empire from his palace in Babylon. He had big plans for his empire. But in 323 B.C. he fell sick. He had a high fever. No medicines of the day could help him. Within a few days, 33-year-old Alexander the Great was dead. His soldiers placed his body in a gold coffin. It was taken to Alexandria in Egypt to be buried.

After his death, Alexander's lands were divided up among some of his generals. The great empire was gone forever, split into separate smaller empires.

But the man who set out to conquer the world had left his mark. The beautiful city of Alexandria still stood bearing his name. And Greek ideas and culture had been carried into far-off lands.

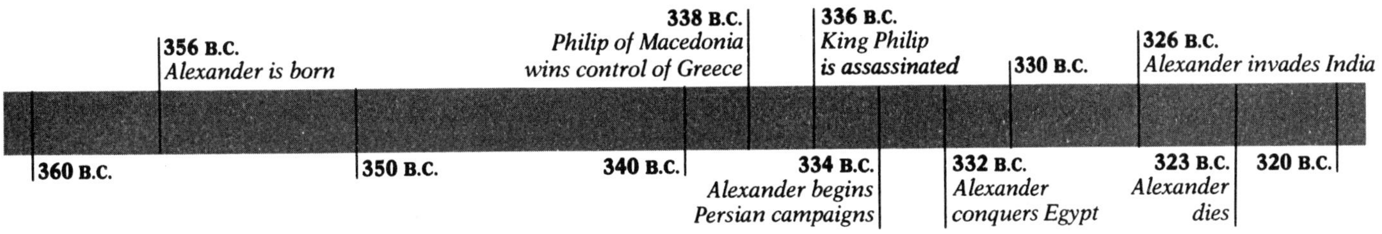

Points to Remember

- ◆ King Philip of Macedonia planned to conquer the Persian Empire.
- ◆ Because Philip needed all of Greece behind him, he first conquered the Greek city-states (except Sparta).
- ◆ King Philip died, and his son Alexander led the Macedonian armies into Persia.
- ◆ Alexander conquered Persia and then went on to Egypt and India.
- ◆ Alexander set out to conquer the world.
- ◆ Alexander brought Greek ideas and culture to the lands he conquered.
- ◆ Alexander died at the age of 33.
- ◆ Alexander's empire split up after his death.

Think About It!

1. What did Alexander learn during his boyhood that made him ready to become a king and a conqueror at age 20?
2. Why were the Egyptians so easily conquered by Alexander?
3. Describe the city of Alexandria.
4. Why do you think Alexander is referred to as "Alexander the Great"?
5. What are three words you might use to describe Alexander the Great?

Chapter 9

The Rise of Rome

Words to Know

amphitheater a circular or oval area with sloping sides and seats rising in rows around a central open space

aqueducts man-made channels that carry flowing water over a long distance

civil wars wars among people who live in the same country

elect to choose someone for an office by voting

emperor a person who rules a group of different countries, lands, or peoples

forum a public square in an ancient Roman city; lawmakers met there

freeman people who are free, not slaves, and who have the rights of citizens

gladiators men who fought animals or other men in the arenas of ancient Rome

governor a person chosen to run a province or territory

peninsula a long piece of land almost completely surrounded by water (from the Latin word meaning "almost an island")

provinces the parts of a country, each with its own local government, much like the states in the United States

representatives people who are chosen to act or speak for others

republic a government in which the citizens have the right to elect their representatives to make laws; a democratic government

senate a governing or lawmaking body

Look for the answers as you read:

1. How was the Roman Republic governed?
2. Why did the Romans think of the Mediterranean Sea as a Roman sea?
3. What happened when Julius Caesar and his army came back to Rome from Gaul?
4. What were some things Julius Caesar did for Rome?
5. Why was Julius Caesar assassinated?
6. Who was the first Roman emperor?
7. What were some things Augustus did for Rome?
8. What did the Romans build that still stands today?
9. Why did the Roman Empire begin to fall?

Early Rome

Seven hills rose up along the Tiber River in the center of Italy. Small villages dotted the seven hills. One of those villages was called Rome. It had been built by the Latins around 750 B.C. The Latins, or Romans, were one of several groups of people that had moved down from central Europe. They settled in the Italian **peninsula** around 1000 B.C. Rome was not very important then. But it would one day grow into a great city. That city would become the center of an empire.

From 750 B.C. to 600 B.C., the little Italian villages were ruled by a series of Roman kings. During those years, the Romans lived in peace. They were mainly farmers and herders. But things changed in about 600 B.C. North of the Tiber lived a warlike people called the Etruscans. They decided to conquer Rome and the other villages. The Romans didn't stand a chance against them.

For the next 100 years, Rome was ruled by Etruscan kings. Besides being great warriors, the Etruscans had many other skills. They made many changes in Rome. They built a wall around the city. They drained nearby swamps. And they laid the first sewer. The Romans even adopted the Etruscan alphabet. Slowly Rome changed from a little farming village into a city-state.

Then, in 509 B.C., the people of Rome found themselves ruled by a very harsh king. They rebelled. They overthrew the Etruscan king. They took the government of Rome into their own hands. The people of Rome founded a **republic**.

Italy

The Arch of Titus, Rome

The Roman Republic

In a republic, government is controlled by the people. In a republic, there is no king. Roman citizens **elected** men to make their laws and run their government. Three hundred elected **representatives** met in a **senate**.

The members of the Roman Senate were usually wealthy landowners. Once elected, they held office for life. Some of the Senate members were very old. The people thought them very wise. The word "senate" comes from the Latin word that means "old."

The early years of the Republic were not peaceful. At first Rome was attacked by armies from other lands. But Rome grew more and more powerful. After a time, Rome also looked toward gaining more land.

Roman Warriors

The Romans became skilled soldiers. Every Roman male spent some time in the army. Rome's military power grew. The Romans began battling for more land. By about 270 B.C., Rome had taken over the whole Italian peninsula.

One of Rome's greatest enemies was Carthage. Carthage was on the north coast of Africa. It was a city settled by the Phoenicians. Carthage and Rome quarreled over Mediterranean trade routes.

Rome fought three wars with Carthage. These were called the "Punic Wars." The first clash between the two city-states came in Sicily. They battled for the city of Messina. Rome finally won this war in 241 B.C., after 23 years of fighting!

In 218 B.C. a fierce Carthaginian general named Hannibal arrived in Spain. He brought a huge army with him. He led his soldiers over the Pyrenees and the Alps. Many of Hannibal's soldiers rode elephants. The mountains were hard on the huge animals. Many elephants lost their footing on the narrow mountain paths and fell to their deaths. But most of them made it to the Po Valley of Italy. Hannibal was a clever general. He caught the Romans by surprise and beat the Roman army. Thus began the second of the Punic Wars.

For the next 13 years, Hannibal led his army up and down Italy. He won more battles against Roman forces. But little by little the Romans grew stronger. Finally Hannibal was driven out of Italy. Then the Romans invaded Africa and defeated Hannibal's army in 202 B.C.

Over the next 50 years, Carthage grew strong again. Once more, Rome felt threatened. So Rome declared war and sent its army back to Africa. This time, in the final Punic War, the city of Carthage was totally destroyed.

Hannibal crossing the Alps

During the second war between Carthage and Rome, Macedonia had sided with the Carthaginians. Macedonia was still the most powerful state in Greece. After taking Carthage, Rome sent armies into Greece. Roman armies conquered the Greek city-states. They brought Greek treasures back to Rome, introducing Roman citizens to Greek art and style.

The Romans made slaves of the conquered Greeks. Many of the slaves were used as laborers. But some of the Greek captives were very well educated. They became teachers and doctors in Rome. Many Greek slaves found themselves with kind Roman masters, masters who respected them. Some Greeks were able to earn their freedom. So in many ways, Roman culture was influenced by the Greeks.

By 140 B.C. Rome controlled all of the Mediterranean lands. Citizens of the Republic thought of the Mediterranean Sea as a Roman sea.

The Provinces

Rome conquered many lands. Some of them were very far from the city itself. So the lands were divided into sections called **provinces**. Each province was ruled by its own **governor**. Some people in the provinces accepted the Roman rule. Others were not happy with their new rulers. And they did not like Roman customs.

To keep the people in order, Rome sent large armies to each province. At the head of each of these armies was a general. The soldiers in the provinces were a long way from Rome. They often felt more loyalty to their general than they did to Rome. The generals became very powerful men.

Sometimes the generals and their armies fought among themselves. The most powerful of these generals was a man named Julius Caesar.

Julius Caesar

"Caesar" is one of the most famous names in history. Who was Julius Caesar, and why is he so famous?

Julius Caesar was the Roman general in the province of Gaul. Gaul was a land to the northwest of Rome. It would one day be called France. People liked Julius Caesar. His soldiers were very loyal to him. The people of Rome admired his success. He won many battles in Gaul and expanded Roman control. But the senators in Rome began to worry. Was Julius Caesar becoming too powerful?

They called him back to Rome. "Leave your army in Gaul," they ordered.

Indeed, Caesar did return to Rome. But he brought his army with him. It was 49 B.C. The common people welcomed Caesar as a hero. Soon Caesar and his army took control of the Roman government.

Some of the other generals were not happy about this. They challenged Caesar's power. This led to **civil wars**, with one Roman army fighting another.

Julius Caesar was always the winner. He won battles in Greece, in Spain, and in North Africa. While fighting in Egypt, Caesar met the beautiful Egyptian princess, Cleopatra. He found time to fall in love with her. He helped her win the throne of Egypt.

By 45 B.C. Caesar controlled the Roman world. The people hailed him as their ruler. For the most part he used his power wisely. He made citizens of many of the people in the provinces. He even allowed some to sit in the Senate. He made sure the governors ruled the provinces fairly. Caesar made more jobs for the people of Rome. He set up colonies where poor Romans could start their own farms.

Caesar even improved the Roman calendar. He changed it to a system that marked 365 days in a year. He added in an extra day every fourth year, thereby creating "leap year." The new calendar was much better than the old one.

And so the people of Rome cheered Caesar. They stamped his picture on Roman coins and built a temple in his name. At the Roman **Forum,** Mark Anthony offered Caesar the crown of king. Mark Anthony was a senator and Caesar's friend. Caesar refused the crown.

Julius Caesar

Death to Caesar

But many of Rome's leading citizens were worried. It didn't help that Caesar had not accepted the crown. They were still afraid he planned to make himself a king. They were afraid he would put an end to the Republic.

Some of the Roman senators, led by Brutus and Cassius, made a plan. They plotted to kill Caesar. Many of these men had been Caesar's friends. But they did not want to lose the Republic. Their first loyalty was to Rome. On March 15, 44 B.C., Julius Caesar was stabbed to death as he entered the Roman Senate.

The Emperor Augustus

Even though Julius Caesar was dead, the days of the Roman Republic were numbered. Most of the people had been happy under Caesar. They wanted a ruler who would continue with Caesar's policies and plans.

Once again there was a struggle for power, and civil wars shook Rome. First Brutus and Cassius fought against Mark Anthony and Octavian. Mark Anthony and Octavian had remained loyal to Caesar. When Octavian and Mark Anthony won, they turned against each other.

Mark Anthony fell in love with none other than Egypt's Cleopatra. They were determined to rule Rome together. But they were defeated by Octavian. The defeat led Anthony and Cleopatra to kill themselves.

Now Octavian ruled all the Roman world. It was the beginning of a new age for Rome. It was the start of the Roman Empire. Octavian became Rome's first **emperor.**

Emperor Augustus

An emperor had even more power than a king. To his people, he was only one step below a god. In 27 B.C. the Roman Senate gave Octavian the title of "Augustus." The title meant that he was above all other men. He was to be worshiped.

The Roman Senate continued to meet, but the Republic was as dead as Caesar. Augustus chose new senators to make his laws. Augustus, indeed, held complete power.

The Empire Under Augustus

Under Emperor Augustus the Roman Empire flourished as never before. Augustus ended the civil wars. The time of peace that he brought about was called the *Pax Romana* (Roman Peace).

Augustus chose good, honest men as government leaders. He built roads connecting all the provinces with Rome. He improved harbors and made trade easier. Life became better for most people.

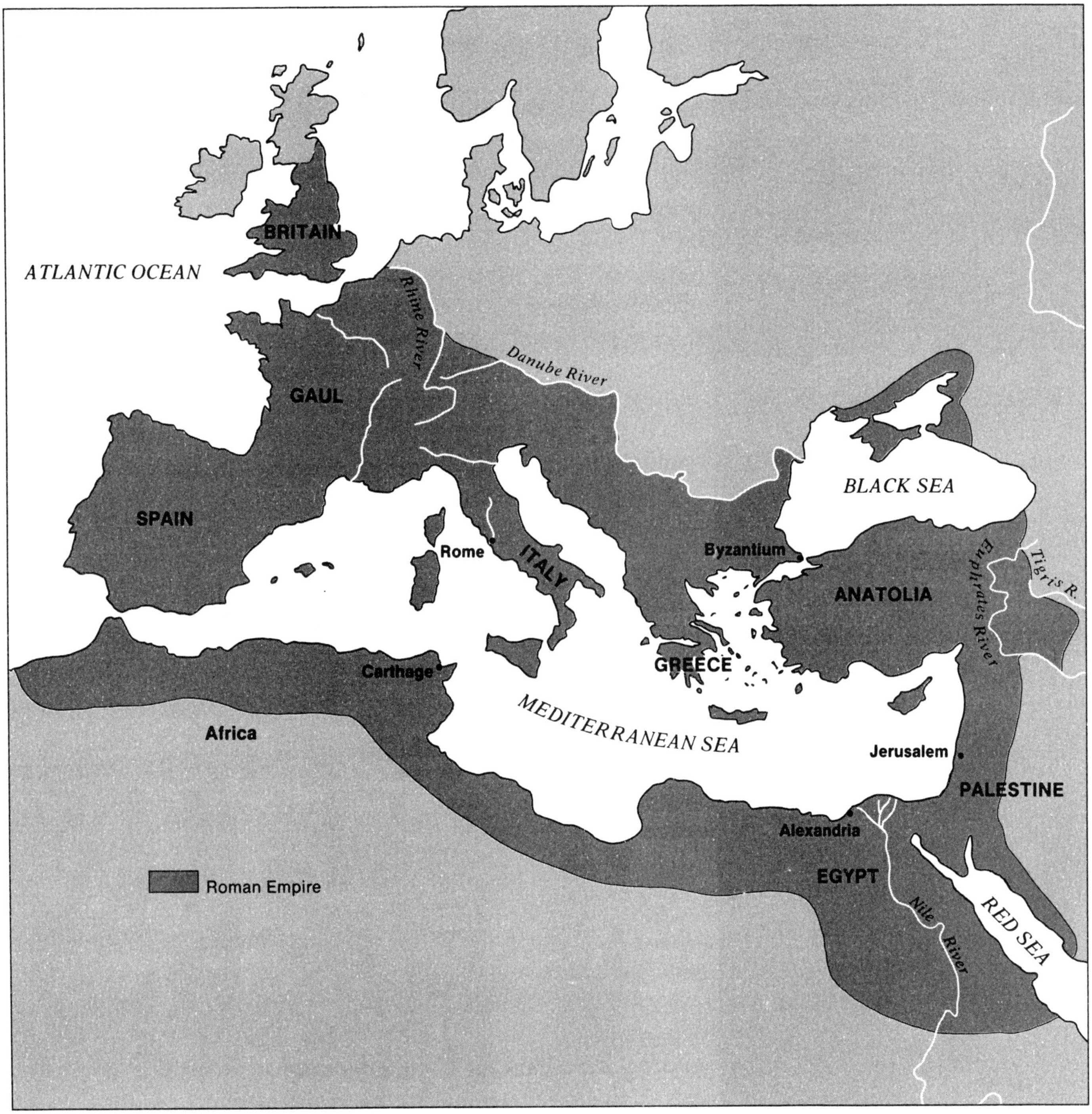

The Roman Empire under Augustus

Life in Rome

Rome was a busy place. A million people lived in or near the city. Rome had come a long way from that tiny village on a hill. It was a fine and beautiful place. The wide main streets were paved with stone. Fresh water came to the city through overhead **aqueducts**. The water was piped into houses and public fountains.

The Romans built beautiful temples to their many gods. There were 300 temples in Rome alone. One of the most famous of these was the Pantheon.

The Roman Forum was a gathering place. It was there that the Senate met in the Senate House. Columned temples lined the edges of the Forum. Merchants built shops there.

The Romans also built huge public baths. They were more than a place to bathe in hot and cold pools. The baths were also a center of social life. The baths held libraries, gymnasiums, and even small theaters. The public baths were free to everyone.

Wealthy Romans lived in big houses. These houses had swimming pools and large dining halls for parties. Many rich people also had country homes. They hired workers to live there and look after the land.

The average Roman family lived in a small house or apartment. The poorer people lived in tiny rooms in big apartment buildings. They often had to struggle for enough to eat.

But rich and poor alike enjoyed the free entertainment provided by the emperors. The Romans celebrated many holidays—to honor their gods or to honor military heroes. On these days they often held chariot races. These exciting races took place at a sports stadium called the Circus Maximus. The Romans loved to watch these events. They also enjoyed a much more violent form of entertainment.

The Gladiators

A huge **amphitheater** stood in Rome. It was called the Colosseum. It looked a lot like a football stadium. The Roman Colosseum could hold over 45,000 people. Crowds often came there to watch contests of strength. These contests were fights to the death! Sometimes the fights were between two wild animals, perhaps a lion and a tiger. Other times, the fights were between men and animals. More often the fights were between men. The men who fought in the Colosseum were called **gladiators**. Most of the gladiators were slaves. But some were **freemen** who fought for money and for glory.

Sometimes it was up to the audience to decide if a gladiator was to live or die. They voted with cheers or boos. The fights were usually bloody. Red sand covered the arena floor. The sand was colored red to hide the blood that was shed there.

The Colosseum, Rome

Roman Builders

The Romans admired the Greeks. They put up statues taken from Greek city-states. They copied Greek style in statues of their own. Many of the great buildings in Rome were also based on Greek style and form.

Roman builders liked to use arches. Arches spanned streets, supported bridges, and held up great aqueducts. Visitors often passed under a great arch in order to enter a Roman city.

The Romans wanted their art and architecture to be useful. The 14 aqueducts that carried water into Rome were certainly beautiful. But they were also useful. And they were built to last. Some aqueducts, built more than 2,000 years ago, still stand today.

Some roads of ancient Rome are still in use today, too. "All roads lead to Rome," a famous saying goes. That means that Roman highways, paved layer upon layer, linked all the provinces to Rome. The Romans were fine builders. They built a sewer system to serve ancient Rome. Parts of it are still being used in the modern city.

Ancient Roman aqueduct

Roman Language and Law

Italian, French, Spanish, Portuguese, and Rumanian are all called Romance languages. They all come from Latin, the language of the Romans.

There are many words that we have taken from the Romans. We have "colosseums" today. Our government has a "senate." The Russians changed the word "Caesar" to "Tzar," the Germans to "Kaiser."

"Justice for all!" was an idea that came from the Roman Senate. Many of our ideas about laws and courts of law came from the Romans. Roman laws and lawmaking served as a model for many other nations.

The End of the Empire

Not all of the emperors that followed Augustus were wise and good. Indeed, some were mad with power. Some were greedy. Royal families often fought among themselves over who would get the throne. But there were always skilled men to do the actual work of running the empire. The *Pax Romana* lasted for two centuries. During that time there were no serious threats to Rome's power.

But around A.D. 180, things began to go wrong. The Roman world faced invaders from northern Europe. Rome had to double the size of its army to protect the empire. A bigger army meant higher taxes—taxes that people could not pay! Prices of goods rose. Trading fell off. People were out of work. Life in the city was no longer good. More and more wealthy people left Rome to live in the country.

The Roman Empire did not fall in a day, or in a month, or even in a year. But the empire grew weaker with each passing year. Its fall was coming.

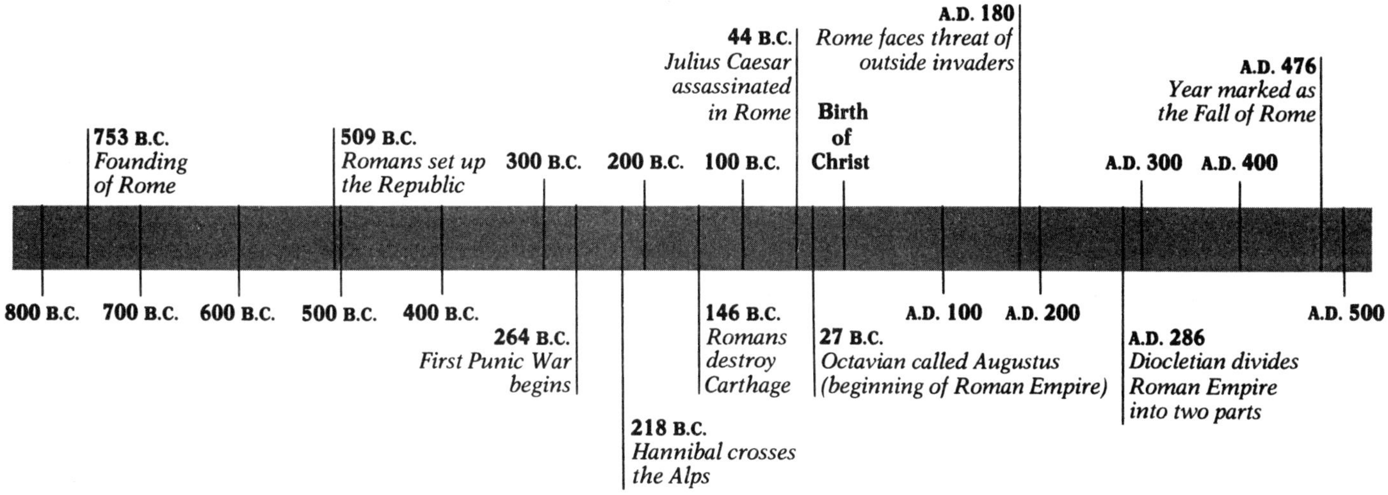

Points to Remember

- ◆ In the Roman Republic, laws were made by elected representatives. There was no king.
- ◆ Roman armies were mighty. They conquered many peoples, including the Carthaginians and the Greeks.
- ◆ Conquered lands became Roman provinces.
- ◆ Julius Caesar was a powerful general in the province of Gaul.
- ◆ Caesar became the leader of the Roman Republic.
- ◆ Some senators killed Caesar because they feared he had too much power.
- ◆ Civil wars ended with Octavian as head of the Roman Empire.
- ◆ The people called Octavian the Emperor Augustus.
- ◆ Two hundred years of peace and growth began with Augustus's reign.
- ◆ The ancient Romans are known as great builders and lawmakers.

Think About It!

1. In what ways was the Roman Republic like the government of Athens?
2. How did Greek culture spread to Rome?
3. If Brutus and Cassius were Caesar's friends, why did they murder him?
4. What happened to the Roman Senate after Augustus was named emperor?
5. Name two things Romans did for entertainment.
6. Give two reasons why the Roman Empire began to fall.

Chapter 10

Religious Figures of the World

Words to Know

bishops high-ranking church officials; from the Latin word that means "overseer." A *bishop* oversees the churches in his district.

converted changed from one religion to another

crucifixion the putting to death of someone by nailing or tying that person to a cross

enlightened knowing the truth

idols images of a god that are used as objects of worship

paradise a place or condition of perfect happiness; heaven

persecute to treat in a cruel way, to hurt or injure

pope the head of the Roman Catholic Church

prophet a religious leader who claims to speak for God; one who tells what will happen in the future

reincarnation a belief that living beings are reborn in a new body

vision something seen in the mind or in a dream

Look for the answers as you read:

1. Why did Jesus' teachings appeal to poor people and slaves?
2. Why did the Romans persecute the Christians?
3. How did the Emperor Constantine help the Christian religion grow in Rome?
4. Who was Mohammed? Why did his teachings appeal to poor people and to slaves?
5. Why were the Arabs able to conquer so many lands?
6. Why did the young prince Gautama give up his wealth and go live in India's forests?
7. Why is Buddhism called a "gentle" religion?
8. How did Buddhism spread in India?

Religion played a large part in shaping world history. Three major religions—Christianity, Islam, and Buddhism—began with men who spoke of equality and brotherhood. Over the years the teachings of these men attracted more and more followers. These religions grew into powerful forces. Today these religions still play a big part in the lives of hundreds of millions of people.

Jesus

Look at any one of the time lines in this book. Each shows how important a man named Jesus was to the history of the world. All the dates before the birth of Jesus Christ are labeled B.C., or "before Christ." All the dates after the birth of Christ are labeled A.D. The letters A.D. stand for the Latin words *anno Domini*, or "in the year of our Lord."

The Christian religion began with Jesus. Jesus was a Jew. He lived during the time of the Roman Emperor Augustus. He was born in Bethlehem, a little town south of Jerusalem. This was in a far-off province of the Roman Empire. Much of what we know about Jesus comes from the Bible. The first four books of the New Testament are about his life. Those books are called the Gospels. The Gospels contain stories passed down over the years.

The Gospels say that Jesus taught people to love one another, to do good deeds, and to love God. If people were good, Jesus taught, they would be rewarded in an afterlife.

The teachings of Jesus were most popular with poor people and slaves. These teachings offered some hope for happiness, if not in this life, then in the next. Other religions, including the Egyptian religion, also spoke of an afterlife. But those religions said that princes would remain princes. And commoners would keep their lowly station—even after death. Jesus spoke of a happy afterlife for everyone who was good on earth.

And so his followers called Jesus a "Christ," or savior. Jesus was about 33 years old when he was sentenced to death. But the **crucifixion** of Jesus was certainly not the end of his teachings. In the next years, the Christian religion spread through many lands.

Jesus Christ

The Spread of Christianity

One man who carried word of the Christian religion was named Paul. Paul spent almost 30 years of his life traveling the Mediterranean world. He told people about Jesus Christ's teachings. Paul could speak Greek. So he took Christian beliefs to Athens and to other Greek cities. Paul started churches wherever he traveled. Even in Rome, Paul found people willing to listen. People were ready to accept a new religion that spoke of equality and hope.

Paul preaching in Athens

Christianity in the Roman Empire

The Roman Empire had many religions. At first, one more religion did not seem too important. The emperors allowed the Christians to worship as they pleased.

But the Christians would not bow down to the Roman emperor. They would not call the emperor a god. The Roman government decided that the Christians were a threat. So the Roman emperors began to **persecute** the followers of Christ. They blamed the Christians for everything that went wrong.

A terrible fire burned in Rome in A.D. 64. This was the time when Nero was emperor. "The Christians started the fire!" Nero shouted. So, many Christians were executed. Paul, one of the men who had carried Christ's word, was one of those killed.

The Romans persecuted the Christians for 300 years! Christian men and women were forced into Roman arenas to fight wild animals. Some of the emperors worried more about Christianity than others. Sometimes the Christians were safe; other times they were in danger.

Christians often held secret church meetings. They met in tunnels deep under the city of Rome. It was dangerous to follow the Christian religion. But even though it could mean death, people continued to join the Christian religion. At first it was only the poor Romans and slaves who turned to Christianity. But, after a time, some of the Roman leaders became interested, too.

The Emperor Constantine

Constantine became emperor of Rome in A.D. 306. In A.D. 312 a Roman general named Maxentius threatened to seize the throne. One night, Constantine dreamed that he saw a cross in the sky. He thought it was the Cross of Christ. He dreamed that if he carried that cross into battle, he would win a great victory. So Constantine rode into battle against Maxentius. He carried a flag that pictured the cross. And he won that battle. Maxentius was defeated.

At the time Constantine became emperor, he had to share power with others. The Roman Empire had been divided into an eastern and western part. In A.D. 286 the Emperor Diocletian decided the empire had grown too big to be ruled by just one man. He set up a system of shared rule.

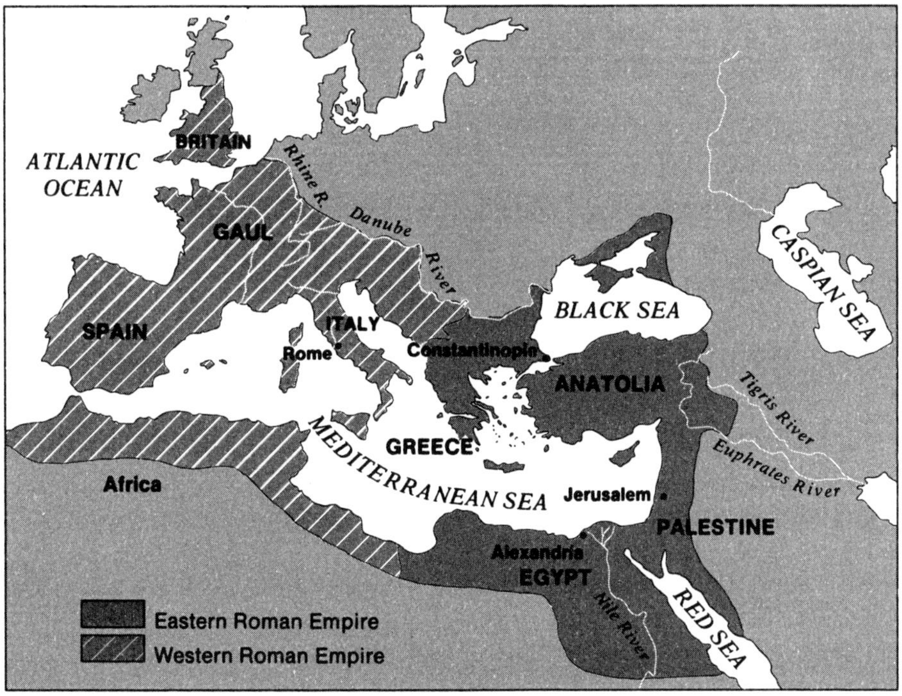

The Eastern Roman Empire and the Western Roman Empire

Constantine was not happy with this arrangement. In A.D. 324 he clashed with Licinius, the ruler of the eastern part of the empire. That same year, Constantine became the sole ruler of the Roman Empire. In A.D. 330 he set up a new capital at Byzantium in the east. He renamed the city Constantinople. Today this city is known as Istanbul.

Constantine **converted** to Christianity and became the first Christian emperor of Rome. In A.D. 313 he made Christianity legal. Christians were no longer persecuted. More and more Romans now turned to the religion. Constantine built the first great Christian cathedral in Rome. He then built churches in Constantinople and in other cities.

The Roman government and the Christian church became very much a part of one another. Officials of the church were powerful men. The largest churches chose **bishops** as their leaders. The bishop of the Church of Rome became the **pope**. While the government of the Roman Empire was weakening, the Christian church was gaining power.

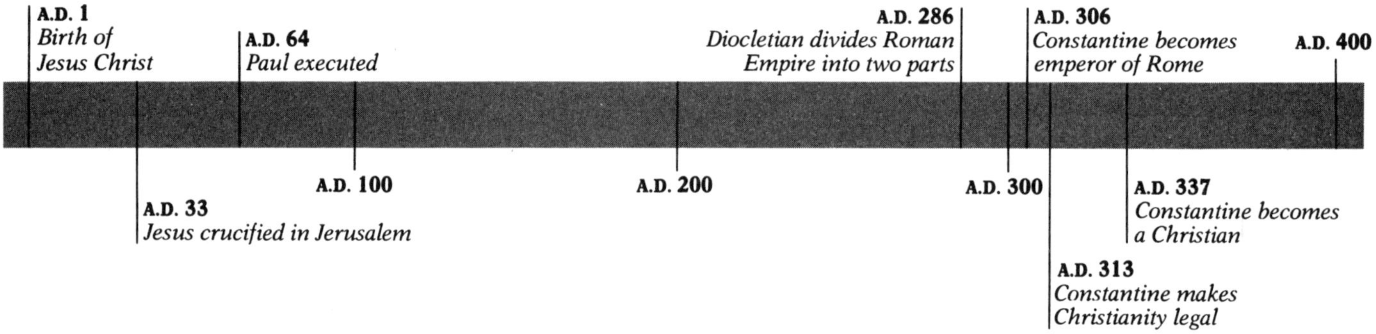

Mohammed

Southeast of the Mediterranean Sea is a vast desert kingdom. Tribes of nomads lived on the edges of the desert in tent camps. They drove caravans of camels across the sands. Wealthy people lived in fine homes in the cities of the kingdom. They dressed in rich silks and wore bright jewels.

It was not a peaceful land. Bands of thieves rode into the cities, waving swords. They looted and killed, taking riches off into the desert. And the nomadic tribes fought among themselves. There was more and more trouble throughout the kingdom. Trade became harder, and the people became poorer. Fewer lived in fine palaces; more struggled for even enough to eat.

This desert land was called Arabia. Today this kingdom is called Saudi Arabia. The people were Arabs. Most of the Arabs believed in many gods. They worshiped **idols** made of gold and silver.

Desert travel

Around the year A.D. 570, in the Arabian city of Mecca, a man named Mohammed was born. Not much is known about Mohammed's early life. But Mohammed was to become a religious figure who would change the shape of the world.

When Mohammed was 40 years old, it is said, he had a **vision**. Mohammed believed he saw an angel on a hillside outside of Mecca. The angel spoke to him, saying that Mohammed was a **prophet** of God. "Teach your people," the angel said, "that there is one God, and that God is Allah."

Like Jesus, Mohammed became a teacher. He tried to teach people that Allah was the one true god. Most Arabs would not listen. They still worshiped their many gods.

But some people did follow Mohammed. They heard his words about Allah. Allah would reward people for good deeds with a wonderful life after death, Mohammed promised. Poor people listened. Slaves listened. Just as they had listened to Jesus, people whose lives were hard or sad listened to Mohammed.

The powerful leaders of Mecca began to worry. They had laughed at him at first, this man called Mohammed. But he was growing popular. What if he stirred the commoners into a rebellion? So they began to persecute Mohammed and his followers.

The Moslems, Mohammed's followers, were forced to flee the city of Mecca. In A.D. 622 Mohammed took his people to the Arabian city of Medina. Still, the number of Moslems grew. New converts became soldiers for Mohammed. With an army of followers, Mohammed returned to Mecca and took the city.

In A.D. 632 Mohammed died. By the time of his death, the prophet Mohammed had done his job. Arabia was united under one religion. The religion of the Moslems was called Islam. The Islamic religion promised that any follower who died battling for Allah would go straight to **paradise**. This idea alone created huge armies of enthusiastic soldiers. The Moslem soldiers were ready to carry the word of Allah throughout the world.

The Spread of Islam

Then came one of the greatest series of conquests the world had ever seen. Arab armies swept through Syria, Persia, and Egypt. They conquered some of the world's greatest cities, such as Jerusalem and Alexandria. The Arab conquests continued for hundreds of years. The Arabs took over lands that stretched from North Africa and Spain to the Indus River.

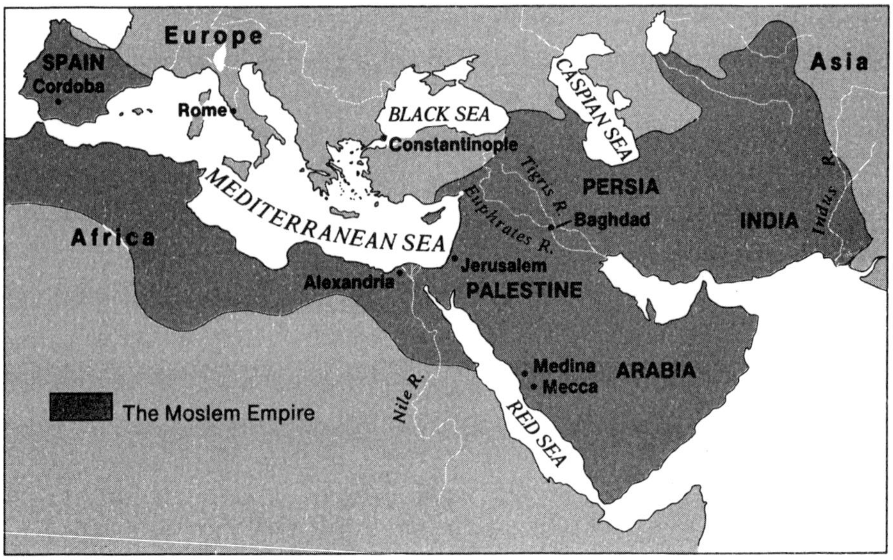

The Moslem Empire, about A.D. 750

Some of the conquered people welcomed the new religion with its hope of paradise. But the Arabs gave them little choice. The people must become Moslems or die. Only Jews and Christians were allowed to keep their own religion. The Moslems respected those who also worshiped one god and followed the words of a holy book. Indeed, Mohammed had been influenced early in his life by the Jews and Christians he knew. His God, Allah, was the one God of the Jews and Christians. According to Mohammed, God revealed himself to man through his chosen prophets. He thought the major prophets were Adam, Noah, Abraham, Moses, Jesus, and, finally, Mohammed. God gave the Ten Commandments to Moses, the Gospels to Jesus, and the Koran to Mohammed. But even the Christians and the Jews were forced to pay tribute to the new Arab rulers.

Early Arabic numerals

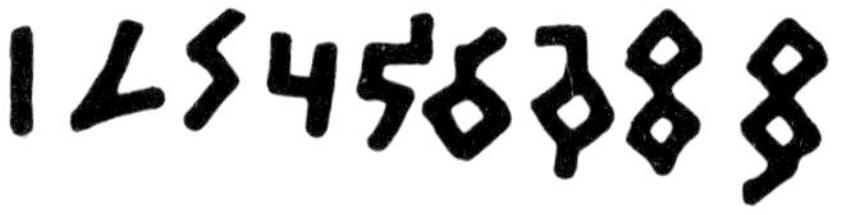

Each number was drawn with as many strokes as the number it represented

The conquering Arabs brought their culture as well as their religion. They built fine cities and new schools. Their language and writing became part of world culture. And so the Arabs made their mark on the world. The numerals that we use now in America, for example, are Arabic numerals.

The Islamic Religion

Today Islam is one of the world's great religions. Most Moslems live in the Middle East, Pakistan, India, parts of Southeast Asia, and North Africa. They live in lands that the Arabs conquered during the seventh and eighth centuries.

Islam is based on Mohammed's writings. These are found in a holy book called the Koran. In it, Mohammed wrote that there is only one true God, Allah. He wrote that all people will be judged on the day they die. If people did good deeds and followed Allah, paradise awaited them.

There are several things a good Moslem must do, according to the Koran. A Moslem must pray five times a day, facing toward Mecca. A Moslem must give to the poor. A Moslem must not eat or drink during daylight hours of one special month called Ramadan. A Moslem should, if at all possible, make one visit to Mecca.

"There is no God but Allah," a Moslem declares, "and Mohammed is His prophet!"

The Mohammed Ali Mosque, Cairo, Egypt

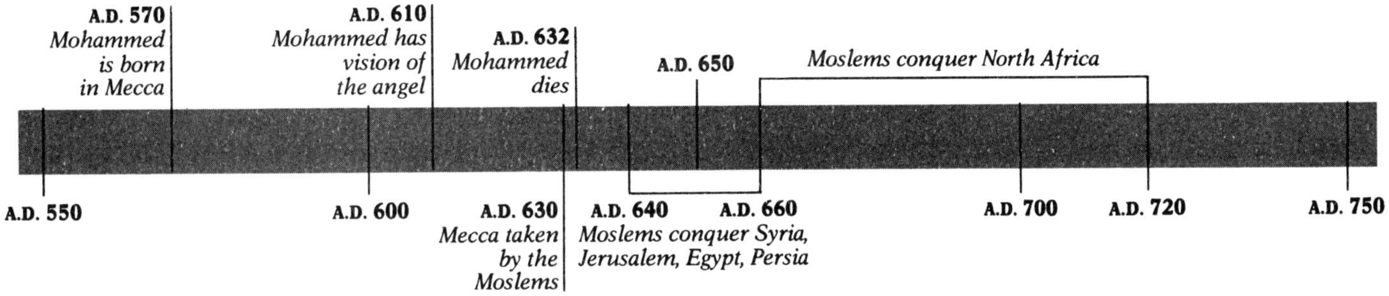

Buddha

The man who would one day be called "Buddha" was born in about 563 B.C., long before Jesus or Mohammed. He was the son of a wealthy Hindu in India. His father was a raja, or prince. And so the boy, Siddhartha Gautama, also was considered a prince. His life should have been one of riches and plenty. But Gautama chose a different path.

He saw many of his people living in poverty and sorrow. He saw beggars in the streets. Gautama felt sorry for the unhappy people. Human life was full of suffering. The rich had so much; the poor had so little.

When he was a young man, Gautama gave up his own wealth. He left his father's palace and went to live in the forest. For about six years he lived simply, wandering around India. He spent his time thinking about how life could be better for mankind.

It is said that the truth came to Gautama one day as he sat under a fig tree. "The sorrows of the world are caused by selfishness," Gautama decided. If people could put aside their desire for riches, Gautama thought, the world would be a better place. So he developed a new religion, Buddhism, based on brotherly love. Gautama was called Buddha, which means the "**enlightened** one."

Buddha and his followers

The Buddhist Religion

The Buddhist religion is known as a gentle religion. It teaches that the secret of life is found in unselfishness. People who get rid of all greed and selfishness will reach a state of mind known as "nirvana."

Buddhists also believe in **reincarnation**. They believe that living beings, even animals, are reborn in another form after death. They see life as a continuing cycle of death and rebirth. A person can only break the cycle of death and suffering by reaching nirvana. Buddhists hope to reach nirvana someday, just as Christians hope to go to heaven.

The Spread of Buddhism

After Alexander the Great had left northern India, a new empire was created. It was called the Maurya Empire. The third of the Maurya emperors was named Asoka. Asoka's rule began in 273 B.C. He followed Buddha's teachings about brotherly love. Asoka made Buddhism the state religion. He taught that all people, and even animals, were to be loved.

Buddha's teachings were very different for the Indians. They were accustomed to Hindu ways. But the Hindu caste system weakened during Asoka's rule. Laws were made that treated all people more equally.

India's Maurya empire came to an end in about 185 B.C. Then one foreign land after another invaded India. Most Indians went back to the Hindu religion. But Buddhism had spread. Followers of Buddha had carried their ideas to China, Japan, and other parts of Asia. Beautiful Buddhist temples and pagodas are still standing today. They show that the "gentle religion" became an important part of Asia's culture.

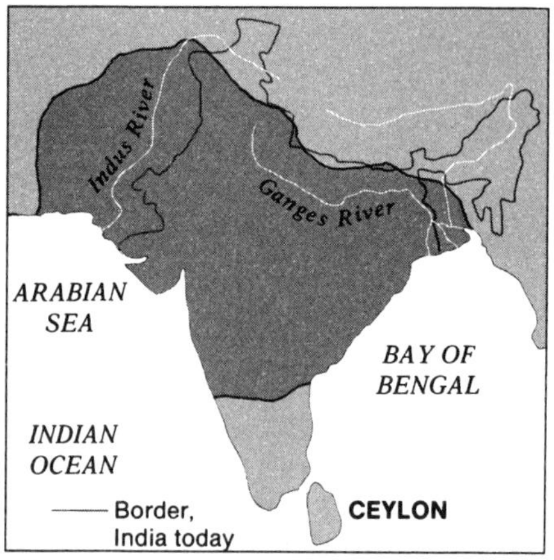

The Maurya Empire, India

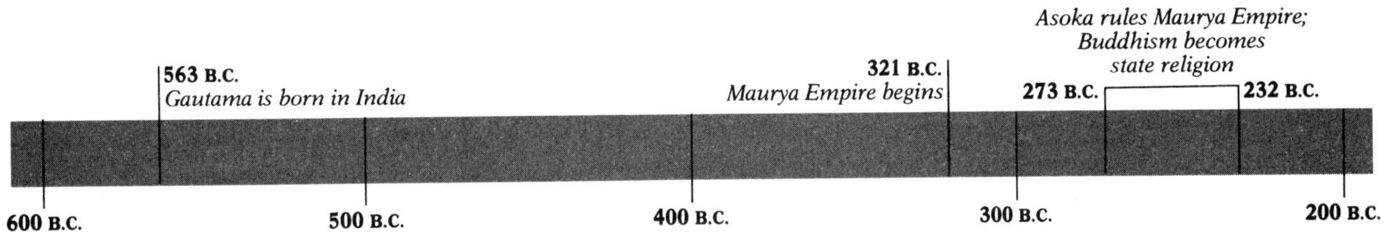

Points to Remember

- The Christian religion is based on the teachings of a man named Jesus.
- Christians believe that good deeds in life are rewarded with a place in heaven.
- Some Roman emperors persecuted the Christians.
- Constantine was the first Christian emperor of Rome.
- Mohammed, born in Arabia, taught that the one true god was Allah.
- Followers of Mohammed were called Moslems. Their religion was Islam.
- Moslems conquered many lands, spreading Islam and the Arabic culture.
- An Indian prince, Gautama, gave up his wealth to teach a religion of brotherly love.
- Gautama became known as Buddha, the "enlightened one."
- The Buddhist religion was first practiced in India. Then it spread to other parts of Asia.
- Christianity, Islam, and Buddhism all spoke of equality and promised rewards for good deeds.
- All three religions attracted poor people as the first followers.

Think About It!

1. Why would wealthy, powerful people at first fear Christianity, Islam, or Buddhism?
2. Why would poor people and slaves be attracted to those religions?
3. What did the emperors Constantine of Rome and Asoka of India have in common?

Chapter 11

The Middle Ages: The Barbarians and the Vikings

Words to Know

barbarians uncivilized, primitive people; people living outside Greece or Rome in the days of the Roman Empire

exiled forced to live away from home in a foreign land

frontiers lands just beyond the border of a country

plundered stole, took by force

sagas long stories of brave deeds

uncivilized savage; primitive; without training in arts, science, government

Vandal a member of a Germanic tribe that invaded the Roman Empire. A *vandal* is a person who damages or destroys things.

Look for the answers as you read:

1. Who were the barbarians? Where did they come from?
2. What are the names of three Germanic tribes?
3. What happened to the city of Rome?
4. Where was the Byzantine Empire?
5. What kind of man and ruler was Charlemagne?
6. Where did the Vikings come from? Why were people afraid of them?
7. Who was William the Conqueror?

The Roman Empire was growing weaker. The tribes that lived beyond the northern borders were growing stronger. The day was coming when these tribes would sweep across the borders. The empire would be destroyed. New people would come into power. And these were people with cultures very different from the Roman culture. A new period in history was being born—the Middle Ages. This period would last about 1,000 years.

The Germanic Tribes

Tribes of nomads lived along the northern **frontiers** of the Roman Empire. These people were known as Germans. The Romans described them as tall, light-haired people who loved to drink and gamble. The Romans called the Germanic tribes **uncivilized**. The tribesmen wore clothing of rough cloth and animal skins. They carried spears, swords, and battle-axes.

The Germans' tribal laws were different from the well-ordered Roman system of law. An assembly of men ruled each German village. If a villager broke the law, the assembly would ask, "Guilty or not guilty?" If the villager said he was not guilty, a test was used to prove his innocence. For example, his hand might be thrust into boiling water. If the burn healed easily, his innocence was proven. If not, he was guilty. The gods had spoken! This was not at all like the Roman courts of justice.

Germanic tribes often fought each other. The men took pride in their bravery in battle. And they had fierce loyalty to the tribal chief. "I am a man now!" a German boy would shout when he received his first spear and shield. To lose his shield in battle would be his greatest dishonor.

The Barbarians

The Romans called these German outsiders **barbarians**. Today this word is used to describe any uncivilized person. The Roman frontiers were protected from the barbarians by forts and stone walls. The Roman Emperor Hadrian ruled between A.D. 117 and A.D. 138. He built a huge wall. Hadrian's wall stretched across northern England.

Barbarians attacking Rome

But the Germanic tribes lived just on the edge of the frontier. They were bound to cross over the borders. So the cultures mingled. The Germans learned to use Greek and Roman letters to write their own language. The Romans began to wear furs, as the Germans did. Many Roman women wore blond wigs made from German hair.

The Romans recognized the barbarians' war skills. Some Germans joined the Roman armies. German soldiers sometimes married Roman women. It was all very neighborly at first. But the barbarians would not be friendly neighbors for long.

Barbarian Invasions

The tribes from the north grew restless. They wanted adventure. They wanted power of their own. They saw that they could take power, and riches too, from the weakening Roman Empire. So barbarian armies poured across the frontier.

Besides being driven by greed, the Germans were fleeing an enemy of their own. A tribe of wild horsemen, called Huns, had swept out of Asia. They were led by their fierce leader, Attila. They took more and more German lands. They forced the German tribes into the Roman Empire.

A barbarian tribe called the Goths marched into Italy. Germans who had become Roman soldiers left their armies to join the Goths. In A.D. 410 the Goths, led by Alaric, entered Rome. The city was weak. The Goths took Rome with little trouble. They destroyed much of the city and stole what they could. Then they went on, leaving the ruins of Rome behind them.

Now other tribes of Germans swept through the Roman Empire. In A.D. 455 the city of Rome was attacked—this time by the **Vandals**. Like the Goths, they looted and destroyed everything in their path. Then they moved on into southern Spain and northern Africa.

Another army of Goths settled in Italy and Spain. Then the Angles, Saxons, and Jutes invaded the island of Britain. The Angles gave England its name. Their language would be called English. A tribe known as the Franks were on the move, too. They settled in Flanders, just north of the province of Gaul.

The Roman Empire fell. Many Romans buried treasures—art and religious objects. They tried to save things from the barbarians. Long after that, people were still finding remains of the great empire. The treasures of Rome were buried in the fields and pastures of Europe.

The days of the Western Roman Empire were over. In A.D. 476 the German chief Odoacer overthrew the last of the Roman emperors. The fine cities were gone. There were no new schools. No one studied art or literature or science. Barbarians set up new states. Their kings ruled, blending Roman law with tribal law. The Latin language changed. It became different in each of the different states. Only the Christian church kept its power and its organization.

The Byzantine Empire

The Western Roman Empire fell to the barbarians. The Eastern Empire, with Constantinople as its capital, resisted attack. The Eastern Empire was known as the Byzantine Empire. It would last for almost 1,000 years after German tribes took the Western Roman Empire. Life in the Western Empire was grim. But the Byzantine Empire put up fine buildings trimmed in gold. A new university was built there. The people grew wealthy from trading.

The language of the Byzantine Empire was Greek. This became the official language of the Eastern church. In A.D. 1054 the Christian church split into two sections. The church in the west was called Roman Catholic. The church in the east was called Eastern Orthodox.

The Franks and Charlemagne

"A giant of a man! About seven feet tall! He had blond hair and a merry face." That is the way a writer of the time described Charles the Great, or Charlemagne. Charlemagne was king of the Franks, the German tribe that took Flanders. The Franks had continued their conquests. They ended up ruling all the lands that would one day be France.

Charlemagne's father was called Pepin the Short. He had died in A.D. 786. Charlemagne proved to be a fine ruler when he became king of the Franks. He conquered more land—much of Germany and part of Italy. He showed an interest in education and in the Christian religion. Charlemagne won favor with the pope.

Charlemagne being crowned by the pope

On Christmas day, A.D. 800, the pope crowned Charlemagne. He gave him the title Emperor of the Holy Roman Empire. Although the empire was called "Roman," Charlemagne was still a barbarian. He dressed in the Frankish style and spoke the language of the Franks. His was a Germanic land rather than a Roman one.

Charlemagne's empire was good while it lasted. He built schools and encouraged artists. Charlemagne himself learned to read Latin. He worked closely with the church.

When Charlemagne died, his empire went to his son, Louis I. The empire began to crumble. It was finally divided among Charlemagne's three grandsons—Charles the Bald, Lothair, and Louis the German. The divided lands would one day become France, Germany, and part of Italy.

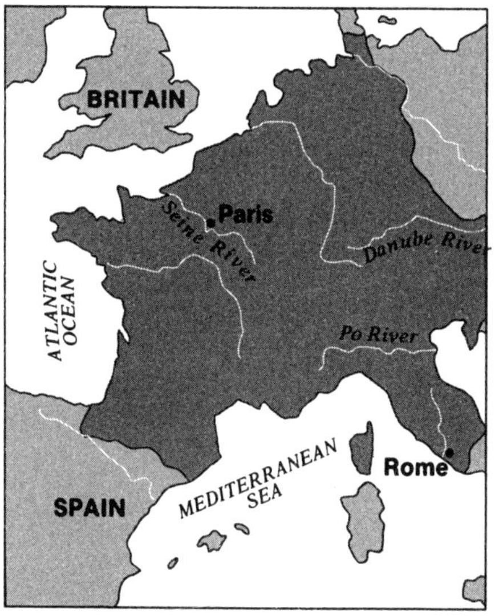

Charlemagne's Empire

"Lord, Deliver Us"

The small stone church stood on a rocky hill near the sea. The people inside were English. They bowed their heads, and they prayed.

"Lord, deliver us," they asked, "from the fury of the Northmen."

The people of the tiny coastal village were frightened. Their town was in danger. Long, narrow ships had been spotted out at sea. The ships' prows were decorated with fierce-looking dragon heads carved from wood. The ships had bright-colored square sails, of purple, blue, red, and yellow. Now the ships were approaching the shore. On board each of those ships were about 30 men. They were tall, blond-haired men, tanned from the sun and sea winds. The men came ashore and ran toward the town. They **plundered** and they destroyed. They killed the men of the town and stole away the women. Then they left as quickly as they came.

People called these attackers Northmen because they sailed down from the north. They came from lands that are today Norway, Sweden, and Denmark. The Northmen were adventurers. They loved sailing and fighting. Their ships, powered by oars and sails, were swift. The sailors set their course by the stars and by the sun. They called themselves Vikings.

A Viking ship

The Viking raids began in A.D. 793. Norwegian Vikings attacked an island off the east coast of England. This was followed by a wave of raids against England, Scotland, and Ireland. During the mid-800s Norwegian Vikings burned and looted towns on the coasts of France, Spain, and Italy.

Viking Settlers and Explorers

For many years the Vikings kept on the move. They plundered, then sailed back home. Later, they settled in the lands that their ships reached.

Swedish Vikings settled in Russia. Danish Vikings found homes in England and along the coast of France. The Vikings in France became known as the Normans. And their new land was called Normandy.

Norwegian Vikings sailed the Atlantic Ocean and set up colonies in Iceland. In about A.D. 982, the red-bearded Viking, Eric the Red, was **exiled** from his home in Iceland. So Eric sailed to Greenland to set up a colony.

Eric had a son, known as Leif Ericson. In A.D. 1000 Ericson sailed as far as the east coast of North America. The Vikings only spent a short time there. They made wine from the grapes they found. So Ericson called the land Vinland (or Wineland).

Songs and stories of Leif Ericson, Eric the Red, and other Viking heroes are called **sagas**. Much of what we know about the Vikings comes from these sagas. They tell of Viking gods like Odin and Thor. They tell of Valhalla, the hall of the gods, where dead Viking warriors live forever.

The Normans

The Vikings in France, the Normans, were great warriors. After they conquered Normandy, they set out to take more land.

In 1066 William, the Duke of Normandy, decided to make himself King of England. He waited for fair breezes to blow his ships across the English Channel. At last the moment came.

There was a savage fight known as the Battle of Hastings. William killed the English king, Harold. William became King of England. He became known as William the Conqueror.

Vikings in the Middle Ages

With new settlements and new languages, the Vikings turned to a new religion. They became Christians, leaving behind the Norse gods of the sagas.

The Vikings kept sea trade alive and booming. They used their fine ships and sailing skills to travel oceans and rivers. Their art is found throughout Europe. They decorated buildings, as well as ships, with carved dragon heads and carved animals.

Because they settled in so many lands, the hardy, adventurous Vikings left their mark on many cultures.

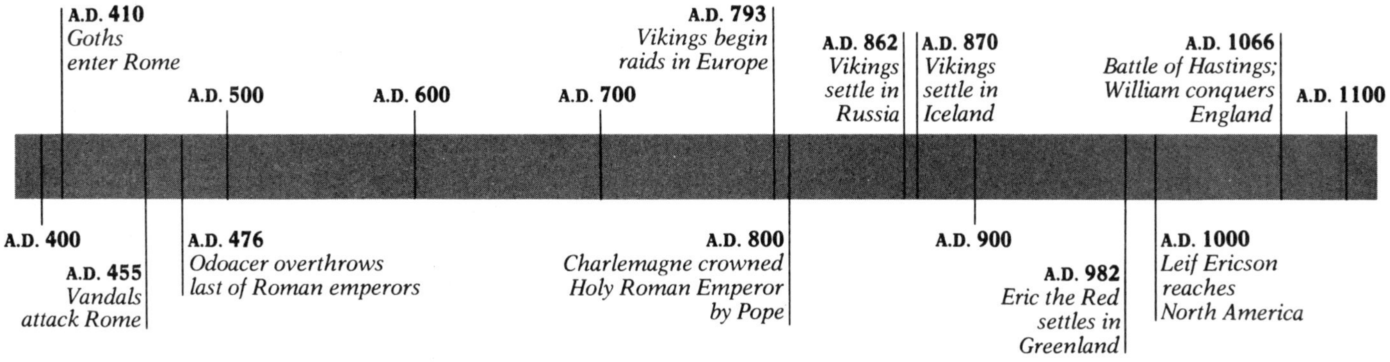

Points to Remember

- Tribes of Germans lived along the northern frontier of the Roman Empire.
- The Romans called those people barbarians.
- Barbarians attacked and conquered the Western Roman Empire.
- The Eastern Empire, or Byzantine Empire, did not fall for another 1,000 years.
- The pope crowned Charlemagne, a Frank, as Emperor of the Holy Roman Empire.
- Vikings sailed to other parts of Europe from Norway, Denmark, and Sweden.
- The Vikings settled many of the places they raided.
- Vikings also had colonies in Iceland and Greenland.
- The Viking Leif Ericson visited America.
- William the Conqueror was a Viking Duke of Normandy who conquered England.
- The Vikings influenced many cultures during the Middle Ages.

Think About It!

1. Describe two differences between Roman culture and the German culture.
2. What high position did Charlemagne hold? What kind of man was he? What kind of ruler?
3. What are three words you might use to describe the Vikings?
4. Name three places that the Vikings settled.

Chapter 12

The Middle Ages: The Lords and the Serfs

Words to Know

clergy people trained or ordained for religious work

estate a large piece of land with a large home on it

feudalism the political and military system of Europe during the Middle Ages; the system of exchanging land for services

homage a pledge of loyalty; a promise to serve, made to kings and lords during the Middle Ages

jousts fights with lances between two knights on horseback

knights high-ranking soldiers of the Middle Ages who received their titles from a noble

manor the lands belonging to a medieval lord, including farmland, a village, and the home of the owner

medieval belonging to the Middle Ages

nobles people of high social rank

serfs people legally tied to the land; farm workers who are almost slaves

vassals nobles who receive land from a king in return for their loyalty and service

Look for the answers as you read:

1. What was medieval life like for the lord of a manor?
2. What was medieval life like for a serf?
3. What were the three classes in a feudal society?
4. How did a boy become a knight?
5. What role did religion play in feudal life?
6. What was "the Black Death"?

The Feudal System

When the Roman Empire fell, most people in Europe moved from the cities to the country. The splendor of the great cities faded. After a time, some towns no longer existed. Trade all but disappeared. People no longer used money. Education and learning became less and less important. Only in the church was there an effort to continue the reading and writing of Latin. The church also saved the writings of many ancient thinkers.

Life was now organized under a new system called **feudalism.** A king ruled a whole country. He divided the land among important men, or **nobles.** These nobles were called **vassals** of the king. In exchange for land, the nobles paid **homage** to the king. This meant that they promised to serve the king. They swore to fight for him and protect him.

A medieval castle

A noble, or lord, lived in a huge castle or **manor** house on a country **estate.** The estate included a small village and fields for growing crops. Freemen and **serfs** lived on the feudal estate. They depended on the ruling noble and his land for their living.

The manor fields were divided into strips of land. Freemen were allowed to buy and farm their own strips. But they had to pay the lord of the manor a part of their crops. Also, they had to promise to fight for the lord. A noble always had to worry about attacks by neighboring estates.

The serfs did not own their own land. They worked for the lord of the manor, farming his land. Serfs were tied to the land on which they were born. They could not leave the estate, even if they wanted to.

The serfs provided every service for the manor lord. They grew his food and gathered his wood. They took care of his lands and his castle. In the feudal system, each class owed loyalty and service to the class just above it.

Life on a Feudal Estate

Very little trade went on under the feudal system. Each feudal estate had its own village and met its own needs. Each village had a blacksmith to make tools and weapons. Each village had a miller who ground grain into flour. The serfs had to use the services of the manor. And they had to pay whatever price was asked for these services.

The nobles and their families lived in great houses made of stone. The **medieval** manor houses were real castles. But they were still very cold and often gloomy. They had no glass in the windows. They had no running water. They were dimly lit by burning torches made of twigs. The damp, shadowy castles were really cold fortresses. There the noble families could be safe from enemies.

A feudal manor

Many of the manor lords had several manors. They lived part of the year at one and part of the year at another. The lords chose managers to oversee the land when they were away.

While the noble family lived in the castle, the villagers lived in small, smoky huts. They ate from wooden bowls and sat on backless, three-legged stools. They could not read or write. Their only contacts from outside the manor came when the village held a fair. Then merchants from around the countryside might bring their wares.

A manor lord could treat his serfs however he pleased. "Between you and your serf there is no judge but God," was a medieval saying. No laws protected the people from their lords' treatment.

Men of the Church

Medieval society was a Christian society. Higher officials in the church were nobles much as the lords of the manors were. Large pieces of land were often given to the **clergy**. The highest-ranking clergymen were as wealthy and powerful as the most important lords.

Men who wished to devote their lives to serving God lived in monasteries. There they spent their days studying, praying, and taking part in religious services.

Knights

Except for the church leaders, every important man in the feudal society was a fighting man. Even the kings were warriors. The estates fought each other. There were bands of robbers to be controlled. Tribes of people from other parts of the country often came looking for new lands.

So men were trained to fight. Warriors of the noble class were known as **knights**. Knights fought to defend their own manors. And they fought for their king as they had promised to. They also fought to protect Christianity from the Moslem threat.

Being a knight was a costly business. Armor and weapons were elaborate and expensive. The serfs had to work very hard to pay for their lord's fancy armor, many horses, and fine weapons. If a boy wanted to grow up to be a knight, he began training at age seven. He started out as a page. He learned to fight and to have the proper knightly manners.

The next step in becoming a knight was acting as a squire. A squire served a knight. He helped the knight with his armor and weapons. And the squire rode with his knight into battle. When he was 21, a worthy squire was "knighted" by a nobleman. The young squire became a knight when a sword was tapped on his shoulder.

Jousting knights

Knighthood was both a military and a religious honor. A young man spent the night before he was knighted in a church. There he kept watch over his armor, as he knelt and prayed. He thought about the honor he was about to receive.

Knights kept their fighting skills ready by entering tournaments, or **jousts**. Two knights on horseback would fight each other with long lances. Their goal was to knock the other knight off his horse. The winner's honor was not only for himself. It was also for his favorite "lady" whose ribbon he wore into battle.

A Hard Life!

The feudal way of life was most widespread during the 1100s and 1200s. Life on a feudal manor was hard. There were floods and years of bad crops. There were always battles to fight. And there were plagues.

In A.D. 1348 a ship from the East docked at an Italian port. Some sick sailors came ashore. They brought with them a terrible plague. This disease became known as the Black Death. It got its name because it caused spots of blood to turn black under the skin. Little was known about medicine during the Middle Ages. There were few doctors. Villages were not very clean. Nobles and serfs alike fell sick. One-fourth of the entire population of Europe finally died from the Black Death.

Feudal society lasted for almost 700 years. But by A.D. 1400 the great manors had almost disappeared. Trade had picked up. Money had come back into use. Nobles no longer received land for services. People moved back to the towns.

New methods of warfare were being developed. Gunpowder and new weapons such as cannons were now available. And foot soldiers were being used more effectively. Because of these changes, knights were no longer useful.

But for hundreds of years, the picture of life in Europe had been the feudal manor. It was a world where everyone fit into one of three classes: nobles, clergy, or workers. "Some fight," a medieval bishop wrote. "Others pray. And others work."

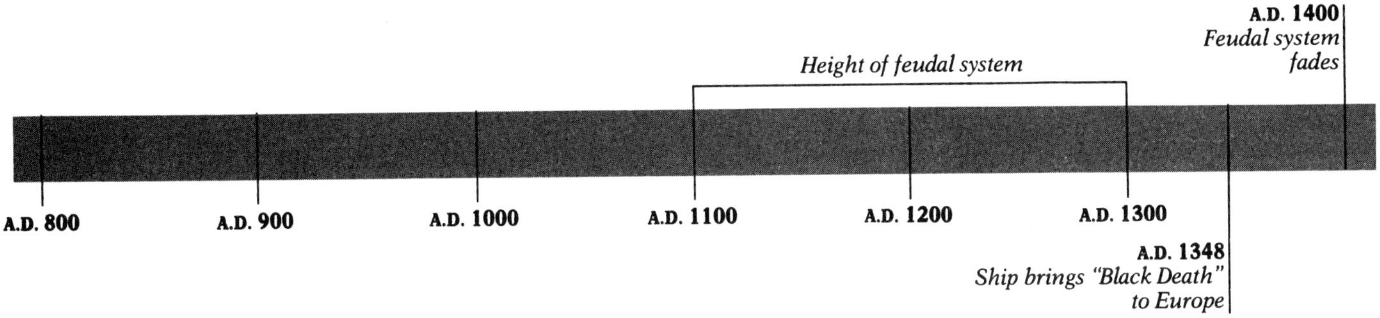

Points to Remember

- During the Middle Ages people lived under the feudal system.
- In return for land, nobles paid homage to their king.
- Medieval manors included a manor house, a village, and fields.
- Serfs worked the land for the lord of the manor.
- Knights were warriors of the noble class.
- Medieval society was divided into three classes: the nobles, the clergy, and the workers.

Think About It!

1. Describe a medieval castle.
2. Could a serf leave his lord's manor if he wanted to?
3. How did a person become a knight?
4. Name three ways in which feudal life was hard.

Chapter 13

The Middle Ages: Changes

Words to Know

apprentices people who learn a trade under a master

fallow land not used for farming during a season

guild a medieval organization formed to protect the interests of workers in one craft or trade

harness leather straps that fasten a horse to a plow, cart, or wagon

journeyman a person who has finished his apprenticeship and receives wages, but who is not yet a master

jury a group of people who listen in court to decide if an accused person is guilty or not guilty

justice fairness according to the principles of right and wrong; what is deserved; the administration of law

migrate to move away from one country or region to settle in another

pilgrimages visits to a holy place

plowshare the broad blade of a plow

population people living in a place, or the total number of those people

surplus more than what is needed

truce a time when enemies agree to stop fighting

Look for the answers as you read:

1. What were some of the reasons people went on the Crusades?
2. After the Crusades, who ended up controlling the Holy Land?
3. How did the Crusades affect European trade?
4. What were some new developments in farming in the Middle Ages?
5. What was life like in a medieval town?
6. What were medieval guilds?
7. How did the growth of towns weaken the feudal system?
8. What was the Magna Carta?

The Middle Ages is often thought of as a time of darkness, of little forward movement. But there were changes going on in medieval Europe. The Crusades, or Holy Wars, brought new ideas and new interests to Europeans. There were changes happening on medieval farms and in towns. Some people began recognizing that kings had too much power. People could see that their rights were being denied. Europe changed very slowly during the Middle Ages, but it did change.

The Crusades

During the Middle Ages, the Christian religion was the strongest force in Europe. People made **pilgrimages** to show their faith. From Germany, France, England, and Italy they traveled to holy shrines. Thousands of pilgrims went on foot and on horseback. They crowded Europe's roads.

Pilgrims traveled east to the Holy City of Jerusalem. Jerusalem had been a holy city for the Jews since the days of Solomon's splendid temple. Now it was a holy city for the Christians as well. Christian pilgrims flocked to Jerusalem. They went to see the place where Jesus had lived and taught.

The Moslems called Jerusalem a holy city, too. And Jerusalem was then under Arabic control. The Arabs respected the Christian religion. They allowed Christian pilgrims to visit the Moslem city.

But, in 1071, the Seljuk Turks took power in Jerusalem. The Turks were Moslems, too. But they were not as friendly to the Christians. The Turks would not allow Christians to visit their city. They would not let them worship at the holy shrines.

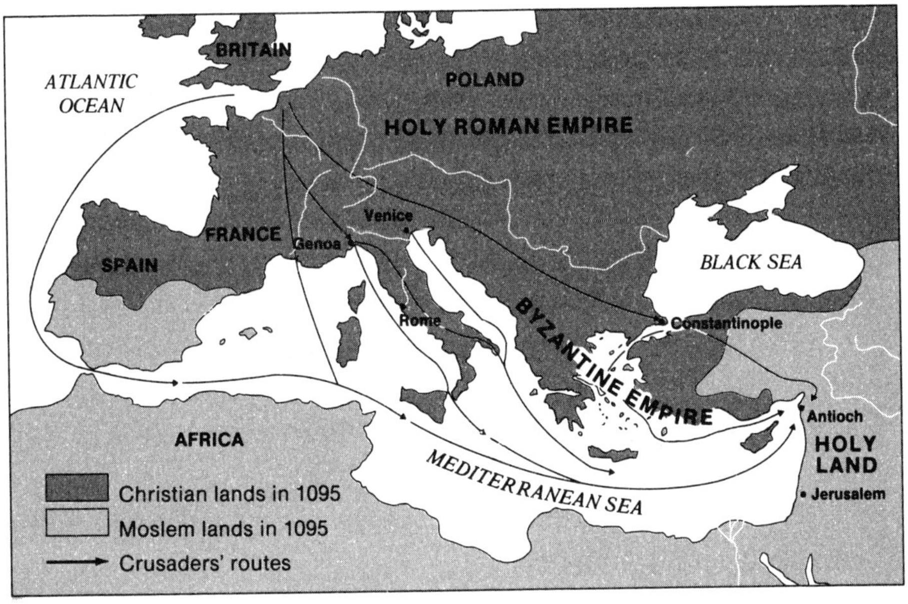

The Crusades

The Soldiers of Christ

An angry pope, named Urban II, stirred Europeans to action. He spoke before a gathering of important people. He reminded them that the Turks held Jerusalem. He told them that Christians there were in danger. It was their Christian duty, he said, to free the Holy Land.

People listened. Feudal nobles, knights, and commoners were all moved to action. Word spread across Europe. Soon armies of Christians were ready to travel to the Holy Land. They wore a cross sewed on their clothing as a symbol of their mission. Then the Christian armies set forth on the Crusades. The holy wars they started were to last for 200 years.

Many crusaders marched because of strong religious feelings. But some went on the Crusades for other reasons. Some were looking for adventure. Others were looking for wealth in new lands. Soldiers wanted military glory. Merchants wanted new markets for their goods. Criminals wanted a safe place to hide.

Crusaders came from every social class—kings and nobles, knights and lords. They all set out to take Jerusalem from the Moslems. The serfs saw a chance to escape feudal manors. They joined the march, too.

Off to the Crusades

Crusaders in battle

The earliest Crusade, in 1096, was led by a man called Peter the Hermit. These first crusaders were a ragtag bunch of unorganized peasants. They started off for the Holy Land before the huge armies of knights did. They did not do very well. They had to steal food along the way to keep from starving. The Turks had little trouble defeating them. Most were killed before they ever reached Jerusalem.

In the autumn of 1096, several armies of knights set out from Europe. Nobles from France led the march. It was a hard trip. Over the next two years, many died from hunger and from disease. The knights had to fight many battles along the way. But those who made it to Jerusalem were ready for another fight. They started a bloody battle. It lasted six weeks. When it was over, the crusaders had taken Jerusalem from the Moslems. The crusaders had killed many of the people who lived there—Jews as well as Moslems. The year was 1099.

The noblemen from Europe set up several small states in the Holy Land. Christians back home were pleased. The Holy Land was under Christian control. Most of the crusaders returned to Europe.

Then European leaders in Jerusalem began to quarrel among themselves. The Turks launched new attacks. So more crusaders went off to help protect the Holy Land.

A Truce

The Moslems had a leader who was said to be strong and wise. His name was Saladin. Saladin's troops won back the city of Jerusalem in 1187.

Then European rulers joined together to fight for the Holy City. Three of them set off on a Crusade. They were the German emperor, Frederick I (called Barbarossa), King Philip II of France (called Philip Augustus), and King Richard I of England (Richard the Lion-Hearted). Together they went to fight for Jerusalem.

The German emperor, Frederick, accidentally drowned on the trip to the Middle East. King Philip of France returned home before the Crusade was over. He claimed he was too sick to fight. It was up to Richard the Lion-Hearted to face Saladin.

Richard and Saladin were both great leaders and great warriors. They had great respect for each other's skills. When they met in battle, Saladin's forces gained the upper hand. Then word came that Richard was needed back in England. Saladin agreed to a five-year **truce**. Under the terms of the truce, Christians would be allowed to visit Jerusalem. And they could also keep control of a few cities on the coast.

But Saladin died, and the truce weakened. By 1291 the Moslems again held all of the Holy Land. In 1453 the Ottoman Turks took power in Turkey. The Holy Land fell under their rule. The Ottomans also put an end to the Byzantine Empire. They changed the name of their capital city, Constantinople, to Istanbul. By 1500 the Ottomans would rule over a huge empire. The Middle East, North Africa, and much of eastern Europe fell to the Ottomans. The Ottoman Empire would last for hundreds of years.

The Children's Crusade

Europeans found the Crusades costly in many ways. It took a lot of money to equip the warriors and send them such great distances. And the Crusades were also costly in terms of lives. Many people, both Christians and Moslems, died bloody deaths fighting for the Holy Land. In the name of God, people had looted, burned, and killed.

One of the saddest of the Crusades became known as the Children's Crusade. In 1212 an army of 30,000 French boys and girls set out to fight. Most of them were twelve years old or younger. They were gathered together and led by a shepherd boy named Stephen.

At first it must have seemed like an adventure for the children. But it ended badly. Nearly all of the 30,000 children died. Most fell sick along the way, or they starved to death.

Another army of German youths headed for Jerusalem. Led by a boy named Nicholas, these 20,000 children never saw the Holy Land either. When seven ships offered to take them to Jerusalem, they accepted. How lucky, they thought, to get a ride!

But it turned out to be bad luck indeed. Two of the ships were wrecked in storms. All of the children aboard drowned. The rest of the ships were not headed for Jerusalem at all. The children had been tricked. The ships took them to Egypt where they were sold as slaves.

In the beginning, people thought the Crusades would lead them to glory. But the Holy Wars only caused suffering and misery. And this was all in the name of religions based on brotherhood and love.

The Crusades Bring Change to Europe

By 1291 the Christians had lost all of the lands they once held in the Middle East. But the Crusades of the Middle Ages had created a new Europe.

Crusaders brought back Middle Eastern ideas. Crusading merchants brought home new products. They introduced Europe to foods like lemons, rice, apricots, and melons. New spices like ginger and pepper, cloves and cinnamon, now seasoned European food. The merchants brought fine cloth. Europeans began wearing brightly dyed silks. With the new trading, Europe's whole economy became stronger.

When the Crusaders left Europe, their journeys gave them fresh ideas. There was a new interest in travel and exploration. People learned to make better maps. All the fighting that went on encouraged even more interest in warfare. Crusaders returned with new weapons and better battle skills.

The feudal society had kept medieval people tied down to the manors. The Crusades sent them out into the world. The Crusades were sad and costly. But they increased trade and brought a sharing of cultures.

Changes in Agriculture

The world's first agricultural revolution had taken place long ago. It occurred along the Mediterranean Sea when people began planting seeds and raising animals. During the Middle Ages another farming revolution was going on. Now people were learning new and better methods of growing food. And these changes in agriculture changed society as a whole.

New Tools

The Emperor Charlemagne had opened new iron mines. With more iron available, farm tools improved. Now there were new metal axes and hoes.

But the new tool that most changed farming in the Middle Ages was the **plowshare**. Early plows had been little more than large sticks. These sticks were dragged across the ground by one or two oxen. They only scratched the earth. It took hours and hours of work to break up even a small field.

The new plowshare was made of sharp, curved iron. The plow itself was fastened to a heavy, wheeled frame. It took eight oxen to pull the plowshare. With the new, heavier equipment, farmers could till even the heaviest soil. Working in long, narrow strips, they could plow the land more quickly.

The plowshare meant that more land could be farmed and more food could be grown. People did not have to eat all that they grew. They had a **surplus** of food now. And they could use this surplus to trade for other goods.

Medieval farming

Horses

Medieval farmers discovered that horses were better workers than oxen. Horses could work longer without rest. They moved faster. With more iron around, it was easy to make enough horseshoes.

Medieval farmers invented a new kind of **harness** for their horses. The new harness fit over the horse's shoulders instead of across its chest. Now the horse could breathe easier. And it could pull heavier weights. It took fewer horses than oxen to pull the new, wheeled plowshare.

Crop Rotation

Farmers learned to get more out of their fields. They maintained three fields now. They planted one field in the autumn and one in the spring. A third field lay **fallow** each season. Each field was given a season to be fallow. This let the soil rest and grow rich again.

The three-field method of crop rotation worked well. If one crop failed, there was always a second crop to rely on. More food was produced.

The Population Grows

During the 1000s Europe's **population** began to grow. But more people meant a need for even more farmland. Farmers cleared forests and drained swamplands in England and in France. People began to **migrate** eastward. Germans colonized new lands in eastern Europe. So changes in agriculture meant that people lived in new places.

As farm production increased, workers had more food to trade for goods. Beginning in the 1000s craft workers and traders began to settle in medieval villages. They moved there to sell their goods. In addition to the blacksmith and the miller, there were now new shops in the villages. The villages grew into towns.

Medieval towns were usually surrounded by stone walls. Their narrow streets were often just mud. Sometimes the streets were paved with cobblestones. The towns were often dirty and dark.

With walls closing them in, the towns were small and crowded. People threw their garbage into the streets. There were no fire departments, no police departments, no health services. Most of the houses were just huts made of wood. With these conditions, there was always a danger of fire and of disease. The town of Rouen in France burned to the ground six times between 1200 and 1225! It is easy to see how the plague spread so quickly in such crowded, dirty towns.

But the medieval towns grew. And as they did, the workers, merchants, and craftsmen became more specialized.

People used money more often now. On the manors, services had been exchanged for goods. Now people paid money for new leather shoes, a pottery bowl, or a tasty cake.

Serfs saw the town as a place to win freedom from manor lords. Sometimes serfs ran away and hid within the walls of a town.

"Live free for a year and a day," the rule went, "and go free."

A serf who could manage to escape his lord for that long became a free man.

Guilds

The towns offered opportunity. Peasants could work their way up in the world. They could learn a trade or a craft.

Each trade and craft had its own group, or **guild**. The guild helped set prices. And it set standards for workmanship. The guilds decided how long shops should stay open each day.

A master tailor and journeyman

The guilds also offered a chance to learn. Boys and girls could become **apprentices** and go to work for a guild member. The apprentice lived in his master's house and worked in his shop. He received no pay.

An apprentice served for seven years. Then he could become a **journeyman** and earn wages. When he became skilled enough, a journeyman made one special piece of work for his master. It was called a "masterpiece." If the masterpiece was good enough, the journeyman joined the guild.

Streets in medieval towns often were named after different guilds. "Tailors' Row" and "Boot Street," for example, were typical street names.

The Feudal System Weakens

During the late Middle Ages, business and trade increased. As the towns became stronger, and the merchants became richer, the feudal system weakened. The towns wanted to govern themselves—to be free of the manor.

Some feudal lords sold charters of freedom to the towns. No longer were so many people "tied" to the land. Most towns were dirty and crowded. But people were freer than they had been on the feudal estates. So they wanted to live in the towns.

Big Cities

Most people lived in the small, walled towns during the Middle Ages. But there were a few fine, wealthy cities. Trade flourished in those cities. There were theaters and hospitals, schools and libraries.

There were cities like Constantinople, capital of the Byzantine Empire. One million people lived there. As many as one thousand ships might dock at Constantinople's harbor at the same time.

There were cities like Baghdad, center of the Islamic world. There, scientists studied mathematics and astronomy. Doctors made new discoveries in medicine. Geographers mapped the world.

There were cities like Cordova, Spain. It was called the "Lighthouse of Learning." Spanish Moslems and Spanish Jews studied there.

And there were cities like Venice and Antwerp. Trade and manufacturing made these places wealthy.

All these cities grew during the Middle Ages. Trade kept them powerful and rich. They were centers for art, science, and education.

Changes in Human Rights: The Magna Carta

There was little concern with human rights during the early Middle Ages. A lord could treat his serfs any way that he pleased.

When King John ruled England, he showed no interest at all in anyone's rights. He didn't even treat the nobles very well! Suppose that King John didn't like a certain noble. Or suppose he thought that noble was becoming too powerful. He might very well have the noble put to death.

Noblemen were angry. In 1213 a group of powerful men met in England. They drew up a list of rights that they wanted the king to grant them. They also listed some rights that they would grant to freemen. Because they included the commoners in their demands, all of England supported the nobles.

King John didn't want to give up any of his power. He refused to sign the list. In 1215 the nobles sent an army after him. King John saw that he couldn't defeat the army, so he finally gave in. At Runnymede, on the banks of the Thames River, King John signed the list of rights. It became known as the Great Charter, or the Magna Carta.

The signing of the Magna Carta

The Magna Carta listed 63 demands. Some were very important. These rights led the way toward English democracy.

The Magna Carta said that:

> A freeman had to be tried by a **jury** of his equals before he could be sent to prison.
>
> Taxes would be collected by legal means, not by force.
>
> **Justice** would not be denied to freemen.

The Magna Carta did not bring instant democracy to England. It really gave more privileges and rights to the nobles. All men were still far from equal! But it did limit the power of the king. And it set a basis for the modern jury system. Hundreds of years would go by before everyone would benefit from the justice mentioned in the Magna Carta.

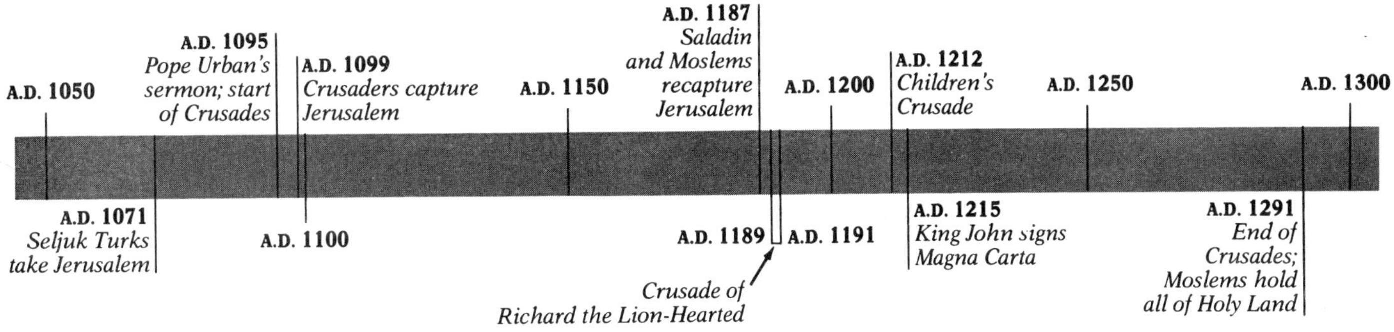

Points to Remember

- Christian crusaders fought to win Jerusalem from the Moslems.
- The Christians won the Holy Land for a time, but the Moslems got it back.
- The Crusades were bloody wars fought in the name of religion.
- The crusaders brought back new ideas, new products, and new plans for trade in Europe.
- A medieval revolution in agriculture meant new tools and better methods of farming.
- The population of Europe grew, and many people migrated eastward.
- Medieval towns saw an increase in craftsmen and merchants.
- The craftsmen formed guilds.
- Most towns in Europe were crowded and dirty, but there were some fine, big cities.
- In 1215 King John signed the Magna Carta, giving new rights to Englishmen.

Think About It!

1. Who were the "soldiers of Christ"?
2. What changes did the Crusades bring about in European life?
3. Name two changes in farming tools and methods during the Middle Ages.
4. What changes occurred in Europe because of the agricultural revolution?
5. What was good about life in a medieval town? What was bad?
6. What happened to feudal manors as medieval towns grew stronger?
7. Under the Magna Carta, what happened to a person accused of a crime?
8. Did the Magna Carta bring instant democracy to all English people?

Chapter 14

New Ideas: The Renaissance

Words to Know

astronomy the study of stars, planets, and other heavenly bodies

heretics people who are against the teachings of a church

humanism a concern with the needs and interests of human beings rather than religious ideas

monk a man who has taken religious vows and usually lives in a monastery

patrons wealthy people who support artists

pendulum a weight hung so that it swings freely back and forth; often used to control a clock's movement

protest to speak out against or act against something

reform to change for the better

scholars people who have learned much through study

sculptor a person who makes statues out of wood, stone, marble, or other material

theory an explanation of how and why something happens, usually based on scientific study

Look for the answers as you read:

1. What does the word "Renaissance" mean?
2. Where did the Renaissance begin?
3. What part did the ancient Greeks and Romans play in the Renaissance?
4. How did the invention of movable type help in the spread of knowledge?
5. Who were some of the great men of the Renaissance?
6. What was the Reformation?
7. Why did some people want to break away from the Roman Catholic church?
8. Who were some of the leaders of the Reformation?

During the Middle Ages the culture and learning of the Greeks and Romans were all but forgotten. For most people it was as if Greece and Rome had never existed. For this reason the Middle Ages is sometimes called the Dark Ages. There was an increase in trade and travel toward the end of the Middle Ages, around A.D. 1300. It was as if a light had been turned on in Europe. It was the light of reason and thought. That is why the period after the Middle Ages became known as the Renaissance. Renaissance means "rebirth" or "awakening."

The Renaissance was a time of new ideas. During the Middle Ages the Catholic church was all-powerful. Thinking centered on God. And most **scholars** were also men of the church. During the Renaissance, people began to think about themselves as well as about God. People used to worry about heaven. Now they thought more about making a good life on earth. This new belief in the importance of human beings became known as **humanism**. The spirit of humanism sparked new ideas in art, in science, in literature, and in philosophy.

Renaissance Art

The Renaissance began in Italy. Then it spread northwest across Europe. More and more people began to appreciate beautiful things. The work of Italian craftsmen became very fine. People thought of it as art. Europeans showed a new interest in the civilizations of ancient Greece and Rome.

"Perhaps," people said, "that is when civilization was at its best!" "Look at the art that came out of Greece," they said. "Look at the beautiful statues and the paintings. Look at the fine architecture of the Romans."

At first Italian artists tried to copy the work of the ancient Greeks and Romans. Then they began to improve on it. Before the Renaissance most paintings were of religious scenes. The people in pictures from the Middle Ages were not very lifelike. Renaissance artists studied the human form. They tried to make their pictures look more like real people. For the first time, artists used live models.

A craftsman could make a good living from his work. But it was harder for an artist to earn a steady wage. Wealthy Italians served as **patrons** for promising young artists. A patron provided food, housing, and enough money for the artist to live on. Because of their patrons, artists were able to work and study to improve. Some of the world's finest artists lived during the Renaissance.

Michelangelo Buonarroti

One of the most famous artists of the Italian Renaissance was Michelangelo Buonarroti. During the Renaissance, people were encouraged to be good at many things. Michelangelo, in true Renaissance spirit, was more than just a fine painter. He was also a **sculptor**, a poet, and an architect.

He earned his greatest fame for his sculptures. Michelangelo studied the human body. He studied the human form at work and at rest. Michelangelo even cut up dead bodies. This helped him understand the lines of bone and muscle. His sculptures seem alive and real. Each muscle is perfect. Each position is totally lifelike.

Michelangelo was born in A.D. 1475 in a mountain town in Italy. He began showing artistic talent as a young boy. A wealthy Italian, Lorenzo de' Medici, noticed Michelangelo's brilliance. He became Michelangelo's patron.

At age 24 Michelangelo created his first masterpiece. It was a huge statue called the *Pietà*. Michelangelo sculpted it for St. Peter's Church in Rome. In the *Pietà* the body of Christ is shown held in His mother's arms. The word *Pietà* came from the Italian word for pity.

"Pietà" by Michelangelo

Michelangelo's statue of *David* is another of his most famous works. Completed in 1504, it is a perfect example of the Renaissance interest in the human form. "David" is strong and looks real. The statue is 18 feet high and made of solid marble. Michelangelo's "David" is very heavy. It took 40 men to roll it from the workshop to a central square in Florence, Italy.

Pope Julius II hired Michelangelo to paint the ceiling of the Sistine Chapel in Rome. Michelangelo painted a series of pictures showing events in the Bible. Over 300 figures from the Bible appear on the 60-foot-high chapel ceiling. Michelangelo had to paint the scenes lying on his back. He lay on a platform held by ropes. He worked on that ceiling for four years.

Later in his life, Michelangelo turned to architecture. He worked on the rebuilding of St. Peter's Church. He took no pay then. He believed it was a task that would please God.

Michelangelo died when he was 90. He had a long life in which to sculpt, to paint, and to build. His art brought light and beauty to all of Europe.

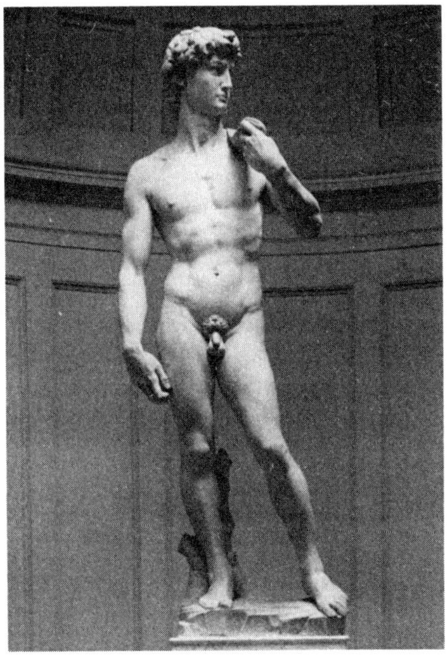

"David" by Michelangelo

Education and Learning

All writing was done by hand during the Middle Ages. Books were copied on parchment made of animal skin. So books were expensive and few in number. Only wealthy people could own books of their own. Most books were written in Latin, the language of the church. The only scholars were clergymen. The church was the only place where any studying went on.

Then, about A.D. 1450, things started to change. Secrets of making paper were brought to Europe from China. They were introduced by the Moors, or Spanish Moslems. Then a new invention made books available to everyone! A German printer named Johannes Gutenberg discovered how to use movable type for printing.

With movable type, letters were molded onto small metal blocks. The letters could be moved around to spell different words. When inked and pressed onto paper, the movable type printed a whole page at one time.

Now books could be made quickly at a low cost. Now everybody could read the stories of the Greeks and Romans and tales of travel. The ideas of the past and the present were there for everyone. Books were translated into the languages of the common people, not just that of Latin scholars.

Johannes Gutenberg reading first sheet from his printing press

With the *Gutenberg Bible* Europeans could read the Bible for themselves. People did not have to rely on the church to tell them what the Holy Book said. The Bible was translated into English, Italian, French, and German.

It became important to be able to read. More schools opened. Schools that taught Greek and Latin grammar were called "grammar" schools. There were new universities. Studies went beyond religious thought. People studied the world. And they studied about their own place in the world.

The Humanists

Humanists were scholars whose main interest was in human beings. They began to question the church and its leaders. A Dutch scholar, Erasmus, eyed the church critically.

"It seems," Erasmus decided, "that the church is more concerned with wealth and power than with helping men find God."

Erasmus wrote books that questioned the church's practices. He believed that simple ways were best. There was too much ritual and ceremony in the church, he said. Erasmus was a humanist. He believed that if people were just shown what was right, they would live that way. Erasmus was among the first Renaissance scholars to criticize the church. But he certainly was not the last.

Science and Invention

The Renaissance was a time for progress. There were some important changes during the Middle Ages. But change had come slowly. Now new books—and new ideas—were available for anyone who could read. Universities were growing. With the spirit of the Renaissance, change came rapidly.

People explored new ideas. Gutenberg's printing press was just one of the new inventions. Inventors discovered how to make springs. Then they made watches that were small enough to be carried in a pocket. Before, the only clocks had been huge ones on public buildings. Now people could keep time at home.

New instruments helped sailors find their way on the open seas. New maps improved travel. People experimented with metals. Soon they came up with cast iron to replace expensive bronze.

In medicine, the English doctor, William Harvey, discovered that the heart pumps blood throughout the body. And in 1600 the microscope was invented. It led to a new look at the world. Suddenly people learned that there were tiny creatures—smaller than the eye could see!

The Center of the Universe

Some of the greatest scientific discoveries of the Renaissance came in the field of **astronomy**. These new ideas changed people's thinking in many ways. Not only were there new ideas about the way the earth and stars moved. Now there was also a new way of seeing mankind's place in the whole system. These ideas shook up the science world and shook up the church, too!

For hundreds of years people had believed that the earth was the center of the universe. They believed that the sun, moon, and stars all moved around the earth. Then in 1543 the Polish astronomer, Nicolaus Copernicus, wrote a book. He said that the planets, including the earth, revolve around the sun.

Most people would not believe him!

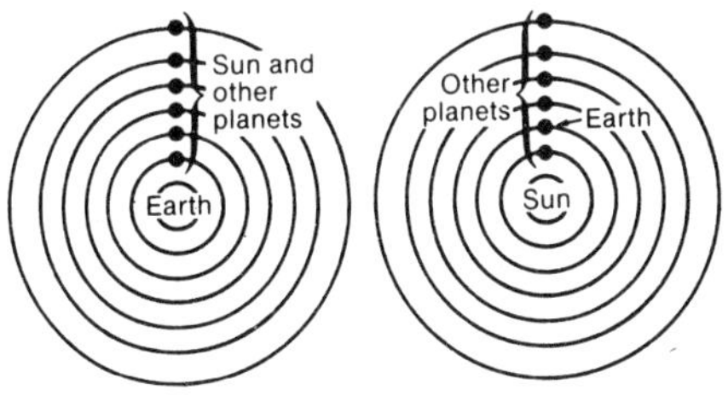

Two ideas about the universe

Galileo Galilei

The invention of the telescope challenged more old ideas. Now scientists could get a better look at the sky. An Italian scientist, Galileo Galilei, took up where Copernicus had left off. Galileo was born in Pisa in 1564. He made his first important scientific discovery at the age of 20. Galileo watched a great lamp swing from the ceiling of the cathedral in Pisa. Then he came up with the idea of the **pendulum**.

Galileo demonstrating his telescope

Later, he discovered the "law of falling bodies." Galileo found that gravity pulls all bodies to the earth at the same speed, no matter what their weight. Galileo climbed to the top of the Leaning Tower of Pisa to prove his **theory**. Then he dropped a ten-pound weight and a one-pound weight. He showed that they both hit the ground at the same time.

Some people were angry. They were shocked that Galileo would dare to challenge the ideas of the wise Greek, Aristotle. Galileo's discoveries would bring him a lot of angry words.

The invention of the telescope brought another breakthrough. Galileo was not its inventor. But he was the first to use the telescope to study the heavens. With his telescope, Galileo discovered that the moon did not have its own light. It reflected light. He discovered moons around Jupiter and the mass of stars in the Milky Way. All of Galileo's discoveries led him to support Copernicus's theory. The earth was not the center of the universe. The earth was just another planet revolving around the sun!

No matter how well Galileo proved his theory, the church would not hear of it. They ordered members of the church not to read Galileo's books. The church sent Galileo warnings. He was not to teach his theories. In 1632 Galileo was called to a church hearing. There was a long trial. Galileo had to promise that he would give up his belief in Copernicus's theory. The church forced him to say that the earth was the center of the universe. Church officials watched Galileo closely for the rest of his life. He became a prisoner in his own home.

The Renaissance Person

A well-educated Renaissance person was supposed to have many skills. Michelangelo could paint, sculpt, and build. Galileo studied medicine, physics, and astronomy.

A Renaissance person was expected to enjoy art, to write poetry, and to play a musical instrument. Renaissance education taught people to read and write Latin and to speak several other languages. People were expected to understand the politics of the day. They were supposed to ride well on horseback and to be good at sports.

A Renaissance man should be able to put up a good fight, if necessary. And a Renaissance person had to learn proper manners of courtesy and grace. Great importance was placed on being well educated and very well rounded. One of the best examples of the perfect Renaissance person was Leonardo da Vinci.

Leonardo da Vinci

A list of what Leonardo da Vinci could *not* do would very likely be shorter than a list of what he could do! Italian-born da Vinci was a Renaissance genius in not one field, but many. He was one of the world's greatest artists and scientists. Leonardo was a painter, a sculptor, an architect, and a musician. He was an inventor, an astronomer, and a geologist. He was one of the first to show an interest in "flying machines."

"Self-portrait" by Leonardo da Vinci

Leonardo's sketchbooks show drawings of many different flying machines. His ideas were based on the flight of birds. These sketches also show great understanding of the human body and of engineering.

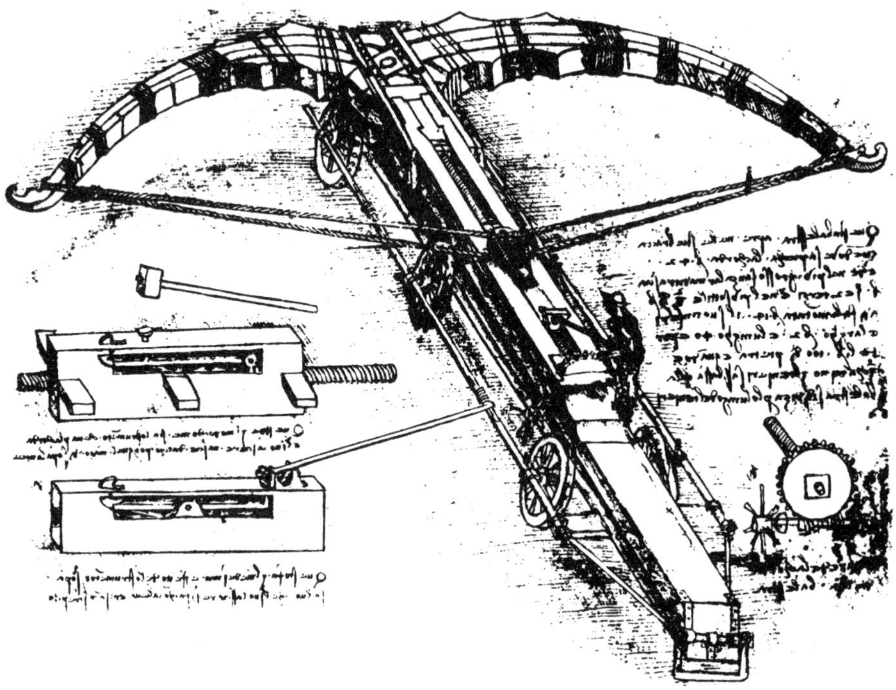

Details from Leonardo da Vinci's sketchbook

He had a sure sense of the way things worked. He understood the way parts joined together to form a whole. This great knowledge helped make Leonardo such a good artist.

His *Mona Lisa* is a painting of a woman with a mysterious smile. It is one of the world's most famous masterpieces. Today it hangs in the Louvre Museum in Paris.

For 17 years Leonardo served the Duke of Milan. He worked as a painter, sculptor, and as an engineer. He was then hired as a painter by the government of Florence. For the last two years of his life Leonardo lived in France. This was at the invitation of King Francis I.

Leonardo, the Renaissance man, used one talent to benefit another. His scientific studies and his curiosity helped him understand people and the world. Because he understood these things, his paintings seemed all the more real. He had a desire to know more about everything. It was curiosity like Leonardo's that made the Renaissance a time of new ideas and new inventions.

"Mona Lisa" by Leonardo da Vinci

The Reformation

During the Middle Ages most of the people in western Europe were Roman Catholics. The Catholic church held great power. The church owned lands and collected taxes. Popes and priests were wealthy men.

But during the Renaissance, more people went to school and learned to read. And people began to question the ways of the church.

Notre Dame Cathedral, Paris, France

Was it right for the clergy to be so interested in wealth? Was it right that church officials should have so much power? Some people also questioned the ceremonies and rituals that filled church services. What had become, they wondered, of the simple ways taught by Jesus?

The movement that questioned the practices of the Catholic church was called the Reformation. Some Europeans set out to **reform**, or change, the church.

Martin Luther

A German **monk** named Martin Luther became a leader among the reformers. Luther was born a German peasant. He grew up as a Roman Catholic. He studied at a university and became a monk. But the more Luther studied religion, the more he worried. His concern was that the Catholic church was headed in the wrong direction.

A person did not need fancy rituals or pilgrimages to find God, Luther said. He began to criticize the Catholic church in public sermons. In 1517 Martin Luther wrote a list of 95 complaints about the church. He nailed it to the door of the Castle Church in Wittenberg, Germany.

Luther continued to question church practices. In 1521 he spoke out against the power and authority granted the pope. This did not please the pope. Luther was told to "recant," or take back, what he had said. Luther refused. He said that unless the Bible itself proved him wrong, he would not recant.

Luther was thrown out of the Catholic church. Emperor Charles V declared Luther an outlaw. He said that anyone could kill Luther without punishment.

Several German princes supported Luther and his feelings about the church. One prince hid him in a castle. The church could not take him prisoner. And Luther had many supporters. So many, in fact, that before long he found himself setting up a whole new church.

The new church, based on Luther's ideas, simplified religion. Religious practices would be based only on what was found in the Bible. In 1529 the Catholic church declared that no one should practice Lutheranism. Lutheran princes decided to **protest**. Because they were protesting, they were called "Protestants."

Other leaders across Europe also protested against Catholic practices. Other Protestant churches were started. The Reformation was under way.

Martin Luther translating the Bible into German

Other Protestants

A man named John Calvin developed his own version of Protestantism in Switzerland. He set up strict rules for Christians to live by. Calvin's teachings were followed in many parts of Europe.

French Calvinists were called Huguenots. But most Frenchmen were Catholic. They began to resent the Huguenots. On St. Bartholomew's Day, in August of 1572, the Catholics carried out a plot. They murdered all the Protestants they could find in the city of Paris. From Paris, the killing spread throughout France. Thousands of people died during the next few days.

In Spain the Inquisition was at work. The Inquisition was a special court. It had been set up by the Roman Catholic church to punish **heretics**. Besides Spain, the Inquisition was also going on in France, Germany, and Italy. The Inquisition hunted down anyone who was not a practicing Catholic. It forced people to confess their beliefs, often by torturing them. Those who would not accept the Catholic religion were burned to death. In Europe blood was again being shed in the name of religion.

The Counter Reformation

Many people who wanted change had turned away from the Catholic church. Others hoped to make changes within the church itself. The movement for reform within the Catholic church was called the Counter Reformation.

In 1545 the pope called a meeting of clergymen at Trent in Italy. The Council of Trent looked for ways to keep the Catholic church from losing followers. The Council made clear just what the beliefs of the Catholic church were. And it insisted that people obey those beliefs. Church leaders needed some way to reawaken faith among the people. So they approved of some new religious orders. One of these was the Society of Jesus.

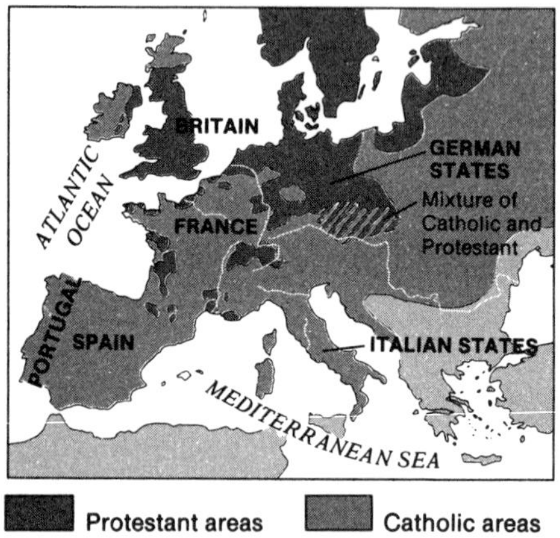

Europe in 1600

St. Ignatius Loyola

St. Ignatius Loyola was one of the most powerful leaders of the Counter Reformation. Loyola had once been a Spanish soldier. He was crippled when a cannonball hit his leg. While recovering, he read a book about the life of Jesus. After his recovery he decided to hang up his sword. He began a spiritual life. He went to the University of Paris and studied to become a priest. In 1534 Loyola gathered six followers and formed the Society of Jesus. Its members were called Jesuits. The society quickly gained many more members. Their mission was to win Protestants back to the Catholic church. The Jesuit order, with ex-soldier Loyola at its head, was run much like an army. Jesuits were expected to obey without question.

The Jesuits did stop the spread of Protestantism in Germany. They carried Catholic ideas to far-off lands. Loyola died in 1556. By then the Jesuit order was well established.

The Reformation Changes Europe

Throughout the Reformation, Catholics and Protestants competed for religious control of Europe. Kings and queens of Spain, of England, and of France became caught up in the struggles of the Reformation. Religion played an important part in shaping Europe's history.

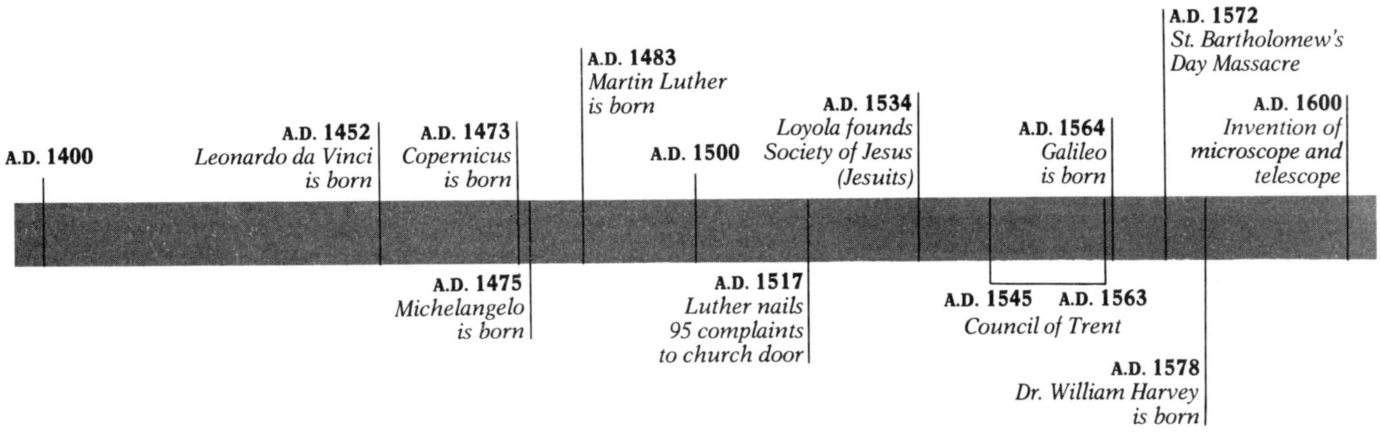

Points to Remember

- ◆ Renaissance means "rebirth" or "awakening."
- ◆ Renaissance Europeans became interested in the art and ideas of the ancient Greeks and Romans.
- ◆ During the Renaissance, great work was done in art and in science.
- ◆ Books became available to all people.
- ◆ Renaissance people celebrated human beings and the human form in pictures and statues that looked real.
- ◆ Ideal Renaissance people, like Leonardo da Vinci, had many talents and many interests.
- ◆ The Catholic church had grown powerful and wealthy. During the Renaissance some people began to question the church's practices.
- ◆ Martin Luther led the Reformation. He wanted to reform, or change, the Catholic church.
- ◆ People who protested against the Catholic church were called Protestants.
- ◆ Protestants struggled with Catholics for freedom to practice their religion.

Think About It!

1. Why was the Renaissance called a time of "awakening"?
2. Name two Renaissance artists who studied, painted, or sculpted the human body.
3. Why was the church angry at Galileo?
4. Name three things a well-rounded Renaissance person was expected to do.
5. What was one thing Martin Luther wanted to change about the Catholic church?
6. Where did the Lutheran religion begin?
7. What happened to Protestants in France? In Spain?

Chapter 15

Kings and Queens

Words to Know

annul to cancel; to make something no longer binding under law

declines periods of increasing weakness

fleet a group of warships under one command

galleons large Spanish sailing ships of long ago, having many decks

loyal faithful and true to one's country or to a person

monarchs rulers, like kings, queens, or emperors

nationalism love of one's nation; patriotism

Parliament England's body of lawmakers

reign the rule of a monarch; or to rule as a king, queen, or emperor

Look for the answers as you read:

1. What happened to the Jews and Moslems in Spain?
2. What goal did King Philip of Spain have?
3. What was the "Spanish Armada," and what happened to it?
4. What good things did King Henry IV do for France?
5. Why did Henry VIII set up a Church of England?
6. Why was Edward VI called the "Boy King"?
7. Why was Queen Mary called "Bloody Mary"?
8. Why did the English people call Queen Elizabeth "Good Queen Bess"?

Spain, France, and England had each become unified into nation-states. Now a separate government ruled each of these three lands. The rulers were **monarchs**—kings and queens who held power over a whole nation.

The people of each nation were **loyal** to their rulers. They felt a bond with their country and with each other. Within a country everyone spoke the same language and followed similar customs. This feeling of pride and loyalty toward one's nation is called **nationalism**. Nationalism and religious beliefs became very important. Both were powerful forces that shaped sixteenth-century European history.

The monarchs of Spain, France, and England followed different religious teachings. Some were Roman Catholics. Some were Protestants. One ruler even started his own church. Because of their separate beliefs, the monarchs led their people into wars. They led them through times of peace, through cultural growth, and into national **declines**.

The history of each nation affected each of the others. The religions and the personalities of the monarchs changed the lives of the people of western Europe.

Spain

In the late 1400s King Ferdinand and Queen Isabella ruled Spain. They were Roman Catholics. They wanted no one but Roman Catholics living in their nation.

There weren't many Protestants in Spain, but there were Jews and Moslems. Spanish Moslems were called Moors. Ferdinand and Isabella called upon the Inquisition to hunt down anyone who was not Catholic. Ferdinand, Isabella, and their Inquisition drove all Jews and Moors out of Spain. The Jews left for other European countries and the Middle East. Many of the Moors fled to North Africa.

Ferdinand and Isabella's support of the Inquisition was very bad for their country. The people that were tortured to death or exiled had been good citizens. They were scholars, doctors, merchants, and builders. The Moors and the Jews left the country. And Spain lost a lot of talent and knowledge.

King Ferdinand and Queen Isabella of Spain

King Philip II

King Philip II ruled Spain from 1556 until 1598. He began his rule as the most powerful monarch in all of Europe. At that time, Spain was the strongest European nation. It held many other provinces. And it controlled rich colonies in the New World. But Philip's reign marked the beginning of Spain's decline.

Like Ferdinand and Isabella, Philip II was a Catholic. He also supported the Inquisition and its methods. King Philip saw himself as a man with a job to do. He wanted to see not only Spain, but all of Europe, under the Catholic church. King Philip's goal was to crush Protestantism.

King Philip and the Netherlands

Spain ruled the Netherlands. Many Protestants lived there. Philip II would not stand for Protestants living under his rule. He issued a royal command: "People of the Netherlands will accept the Catholic religion!"

But Philip did not count on the spirit of the Dutch people. They wanted to worship as they chose. Even the Dutch who were Catholics didn't like King Philip. He was a Spaniard, not Dutch. He expected them to send too much tax money to Spain.

The proud people of the Netherlands rebelled. A Dutch prince, William of Orange, led the rebellion in 1568. Things looked grim. But the Dutch would not give in to Spain. In 1581 the Dutch declared independence. The Netherlands was on its way to freedom from Philip and from Spain.

King Philip and England

King Philip was not alone in his dream of a Catholic Europe. Before he became king, Philip had married Queen Mary I of England. Mary was a loyal Catholic, too. She hoped to see all Protestants converted to Catholicism. Mary and Philip would fight together under the sign of the cross.

But Queen Mary only reigned for five years. When she died, the English throne went to her Protestant half-sister, Elizabeth. Although Philip had been her brother-in-law, Elizabeth saw him as England's enemy. She sent aid to the Netherlands in its fight for freedom from Spain. She gave English ships permission to attack Spanish ships on the world's seas. Queen Elizabeth I was definitely getting in the way of Philip's plans to unite Europe under Catholicism.

The Spanish Armada

King Philip II decided to go to war with England. Philip built up a mighty **fleet**. It was called the Armada. The Armada was the largest fleet of ships that Europe had ever seen. In 1588, 130 Spanish ships set out against England. They were giant ships. There were crosses on their billowing sails. King Philip thought that his Armada could not be beaten.

The Armada reached the English Channel. English ships sailed out to meet it. The English ships were much smaller than the Spanish ships. At first it looked as if they would not stand a chance. But the English crafts were fast. They could dart among the heavy Spanish **galleons**, firing from all sides. The English had skilled captains like Sir Francis Drake. They kept King Philip's Armada busy. The Spanish giants could not stop the quick, little English ships.

A Spanish galleon

The fighting lasted for more than a week. Most of the Spanish ships were damaged. The crippled Armada fled to the North Sea. It escaped the English by sailing north around the British Isles. Heavy winds wrecked many ships off the coast of Ireland. What was left of Philip's once-glorious Armada headed back to Spain. Only 67 ships returned home.

Philip's dream of a Catholic Europe ended with the destruction of his Armada. He had lost many soldiers. The Armada had cost Spain much money. Instead of conquering Europe, King Philip had sent Spain into a decline.

France

France had problems of its own. There, too, wars broke out because of religion. Civil wars had torn the country apart for more than 30 years. The Protestant Reformation had started all the trouble. French Protestants, the Huguenots, fought the Catholics. King Philip of Spain and the pope supported the Catholics. England's Queen Elizabeth sent aid to the Huguenots. In 1572, thousands of Protestants died in the Massacre of St. Bartholomew's Day.

France's Catholic king was assassinated in 1589. Before he died, he named Henry of Navarre as the next king. Henry of Navarre became King Henry IV. And Henry IV was a Huguenot!

"Good King Henry"

The French Catholics were in an uproar. A Huguenot was king! Henry IV had to fight to keep his throne. He won several battles. But he could not bring peace. Frenchmen, especially those in Paris, would not accept a Protestant as king.

To keep the peace, Henry IV declared himself a Catholic. Most Frenchmen welcomed this move. Henry IV was then officially crowned king of France. At last he was able to restore peace to the country.

But King Henry IV did not turn his back on the Huguenots. In 1598 he issued the Edict of Nantes. This gave religious freedom to the French Protestants. It was better, Henry said, than seeing France torn apart by civil war.

King Henry turned out to be a good king. Once there was religious peace, Henry worked hard to make France rich and strong. He passed laws to help the farmers. He built new roads. And he encouraged trade and manufacturing.

King Henry sent French explorers out on the seas. Under Henry's **reign** the first French colony was founded in North America. It was called Quebec. Feelings of nationalism grew. The French called their king "Good King Henry."

But their "good king" was assassinated in 1610. However, the religious freedoms that he had brought to France lasted long after his death.

England

In England in 1485 a man named Henry Tudor became King Henry VII. His reign ended years of civil war. He was the first of several monarchs from the Tudor family.

Henry VII was not a very colorful character. But his people liked him. He kept England out of wars. He was a good businessman and built the country's economy. King Henry VII saw to it that everyone, especially the nobles, paid their taxes.

King Henry VIII

When Henry VII died, his son became king of England. King Henry VIII was the second Tudor monarch. He had a more colorful personality than his father. He is well remembered for having six wives.

The story of Henry VIII and his wives is all mixed up with religion. To begin with, Henry VIII was a Catholic. The people liked him. His father had been a good king. And the new King Henry seemed good-humored and kind.

Problems began when Henry no longer wanted to be married to his wife, Catherine of Aragon. Catherine had only been able to have one child. That child was a girl, the princess Mary who later married King Philip of Spain. Henry wanted a son to follow him on the throne.

Henry showed an interest in Anne Boleyn. She had been one of his wife's maids of honor. Anne, he thought, was beautiful. She would make him a fine wife. And she might give him a son.

King Henry asked the pope to **annul** his marriage to Catherine. The pope refused. So Henry VIII took matters into his own hands. In secret he married Anne Boleyn in 1533. His marriage to Catherine was annulled by the man who would become the Archbishop of Canterbury. Henry then broke with the Roman Catholic church. In 1534 England's **Parliament** passed a law making Henry head of the Church of England.

The new Church of England was still Catholic in its practices and beliefs. But it was not subject to any control by Rome. Henry's break with the church also increased his own power and wealth. He seized all the lands, all the gold, and all the silver that had belonged to the Roman Catholic church in England.

King Henry VIII

Anne Boleyn

Anne Boleyn and Other Wives

But things did not go so well for King Henry VIII and his new wife, Anne Boleyn. Anne, too, gave him a daughter, the princess Elizabeth. But Henry still wanted a son. He wanted a new wife, too. He accused Anne of being unfaithful. He had her imprisoned in the Tower of London. She was sentenced to death, and beheaded in 1536.

Henry married a third wife, Jane Seymour. At last Henry got that son, Prince Edward. Henry married again after Jane Seymour died. In fact, he married three more times. One wife, he divorced. Another, he ordered killed. The sixth and last wife outlived Henry.

"The Boy King"

Prince Edward was Henry's only son. When Henry died, Edward took the throne of England. He became the monarch Edward VI when he was only ten years old.

Under Edward's rule, the number of Protestants increased in England. Protestantism, in fact, became the state religion. Edward was very young. So the affairs of his country were handled by his uncle, Duke Edward Seymour.

Edward was called "The Boy King." He died after reigning for only six years. Now two women were next in line for the throne of England. They were Henry VIII's two daughters, Princess Mary and Princess Elizabeth.

Queen Mary I

"Bloody Mary"

The oldest of Henry's daughters, Mary, reigned after Edward's death. Queen Mary I was a strong Catholic. She was determined to make England Catholic again. First she struck down all the religious laws passed under Edward VI. She made new laws enforcing Catholicism. Mary married Philip II of Spain. Together they planned to put an end to Protestantism in Europe.

History calls Queen Mary "Bloody Mary." She persecuted Protestants. She had more than 300 Protestants burned to death.

The English Parliament did not like it when Mary married Spain's King Philip. They were afraid of Spanish power. They refused Queen Mary's request to make Catholicism the state religion.

Queen Mary I died after reigning for five years. Her spirit was broken because she never saw Protestantism crushed.

"Good Queen Bess"

The next Tudor on the throne of England was Mary's half-sister, Elizabeth. Elizabeth declared that the Church of England was Protestant. The country became firmly united under the one church.

Elizabeth reigned for 45 years until her death in 1603. Her reign became one of the most glorious periods in English history.

Nationalism grew during Elizabeth's reign. Trouble with Spain only served to strengthen that spirit. England's defeat of the Spanish Armada caused all of England to cheer.

Queen Elizabeth I did have her faults. She was said to be hot-tempered. She was also called vain. One story says that when Elizabeth died, there were layers and layers of makeup caked on her face. But the English people loved Elizabeth. And Queen Elizabeth, despite any other faults, loved her England!

Queen Elizabeth never married. Her reign ended the Tudor line. But Englishmen remember her as "Good Queen Bess." She had brought a bright age to England.

Queen Elizabeth I

Elizabeth's England

The reign of Queen Elizabeth became known as the Elizabethan Age. Great writers like William Shakespeare, Edmund Spenser, and Frances Bacon lived in England then. London's Globe Theater was built in 1599. Many of Shakespeare's plays were first performed at the Globe.

Elizabeth helped make her people wealthier and England's cities safer. Except for fighting the Spanish Armada, she kept her country out of expensive wars. So there was more money to spend on other things. Elizabeth made new laws. These gave work to the poor and shelter for those who could not work.

There were ship captains like Sir Walter Raleigh. They brought new products back to England. They brought tobacco and potatoes from America. Daring sailors like Sir Frances Drake captured treasures from Spanish ships. In Elizabeth's name, English sailors went out to explore the world.

The Globe Theater, London, England

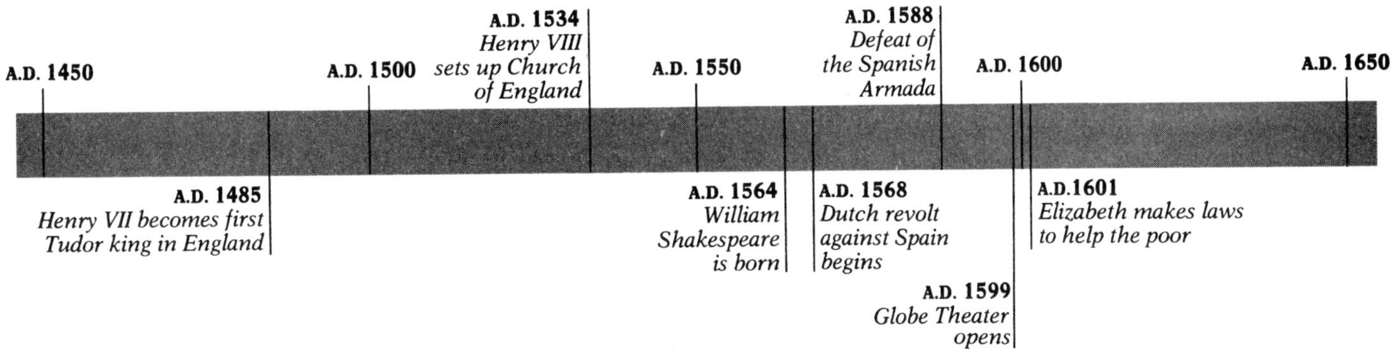

REIGNS OF THE MONARCHS

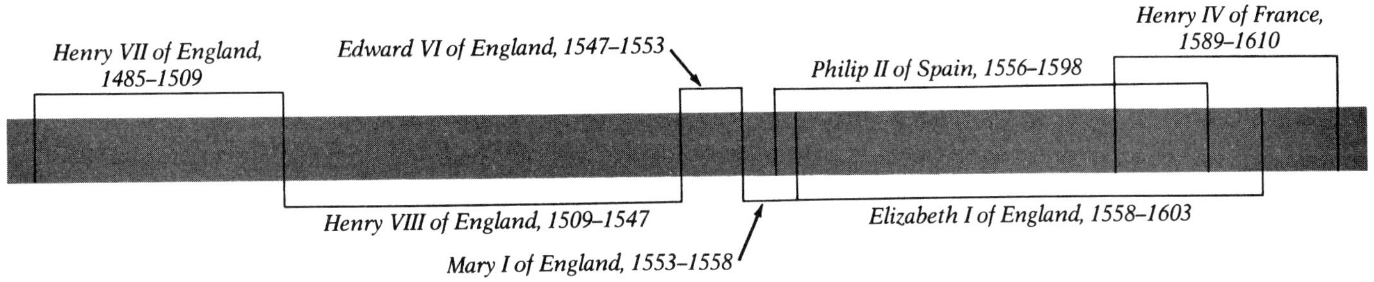

Points to Remember

- ◆ King Philip II of Spain wanted to make all Europeans Catholic.
- ◆ Philip II sent his Armada out to conquer England. But quick, smaller English ships sent the Armada home in defeat.
- ◆ King Philip's reign sent Spain into a decline.
- ◆ The French King Henry IV converted to Catholicism to keep peace in France.
- ◆ Henry IV passed laws giving religious freedom to the Protestants in France.
- ◆ The Tudors ruled England from 1485 until 1603.
- ◆ King Henry VIII of England broke from the Roman Catholic church and set up a Church of England.
- ◆ The last Tudor monarch was Queen Elizabeth.
- ◆ Elizabeth made the Church of England Protestant, and she encouraged English nationalism.
- ◆ During the Elizabethan Age there were many famous writers in England.

Think About It!

1. Different kings handled the question of religious freedom in different ways. How did King Philip II of Spain deal with it? How did King Henry IV of France deal with it?
2. How did King Philip of Spain's Armada boost the English spirit of nationalism?
3. Which of the Tudor monarchs do you think was the most interesting? What do you remember about that ruler?

Chapter 16

Meanwhile . . . To the East; To the West

Words to Know

acupuncture treating pain or illness by putting needles into certain parts of the body

bartered traded goods or services without using money

civil service a system under which government jobs are given to people who score highest on an exam

forge to work into shape by heating and hammering

hermit one who lives alone, away from others

isolated set apart from others; alone

junks flat-bottomed Chinese sailing ships

missionaries people sent by a church to other countries to spread a religion

mosaic a design made by putting together small pieces of colored stone, glass, or other material

samurai a class of warriors in the Japanese feudal system

Look for the answers as you read:

1. Why did the Chinese build the Great Wall?
2. What did Confucius say was important?
3. Who was Genghis Khan? Who was Kublai Khan? Who was Marco Polo?
4. Where did Japan get its system of writing and many of its early ideas?
5. Who were the samurai? Who were the shoguns?
6. What religion did the Moguls bring to India?
7. How did the Aztecs worship their gods?
8. How did the Incas communicate across their empire?

In China . . .

The name "China" may have come from Ch'in. This was a family that ruled China from 221 B.C. until 206 B.C. This period was called the Ch'in dynasty. Shih Huang Ti was the first Ch'in emperor. And his empire was the first Chinese empire with a strong central government.

Shih Huang Ti had the Great Wall of China built. The country of China had many natural barriers to keep foreigners out. Mountains and deserts lay all around. The only border that could be easily crossed was to the north. Enemies crossed this northern border to raid Chinese farms. The Chinese of an earlier period had also tried to protect the border. Short walls had been built by the Chou dynasty. Shih Huang Ti decided to connect these walls. He wanted to build one great stone wall. Work on the wall continued on and off until around A.D. 1600.

The Great Wall of China is the only man-made structure on earth that can be seen from outer space! It is about 4,000 miles long, the longest structure ever built! The Great Wall is 25 feet high and about 15 feet wide at the top. It protected the northern borders from invaders, especially those on horseback. It also further **isolated** China from the rest of the world.

The Great Wall of China

Shih Huang Ti had built a wall that would last for thousands of years. Unfortunately, the Ch'in dynasty only lasted a few years. It was expensive to build the wall. So Shih forced people to pay very high taxes. Many people began to hate the Ch'in dynasty. Soon after Shih died, in 210 B.C., a civil war broke out. The Ch'in dynasty quickly collapsed. By 202 B.C. the Han dynasty had gained control of China.

Confucius

Confucius was born in 551 B.C. For more than 2,000 years his ideas were the single strongest influence on Chinese life. Confucius gave people rules to live by. He was most interested in how people treated each other.

"Never do to others what you would not like them to do to you," Confucius taught. He taught that family life was most important. In China large family groups lived together. Grandparents, parents, and children usually shared the same house. So if family members loved and honored each other, the family would enjoy good fortune. Old people were honored. Ancestors were respected. Respect for the ways of the ancestors kept Chinese culture from changing.

Confucius prized scholarship. Only well-educated people could be government officials. The greatest honor came to a family if a son became a scholar. Then he could study to take the government exams. A young man who passed the exams could become an official.

For centuries in China, people had to take tests to hold government jobs. It was the world's first **civil service** system.

Confucius

Chinese Inventions

The Chinese invented many things. But China was isolated. The rest of the world would not learn about Chinese discoveries for hundreds of years to come.

Papermaking first began during the Han dynasty. The Chinese made paper from wood ash and cloth pulp. The Chinese also knew how to melt iron and how to **forge** it. They knew how to mine salt. They learned to use **acupuncture** to cure pain and disease.

Later, the Chinese used wood blocks with carved characters to print books. Chinese sailors developed compasses. And gunpowder was invented in China. It was first used for fireworks. Not until A.D. 1161 were the first explosives used in actual battle.

The Silk Road

The Chinese kept their secrets. European nations battled each other. Empires rose and fell. But Chinese culture continued over the centuries with little change.

A route known as the Silk Road was China's only link to the Western World. A few traders traveled this road. They made their way across deserts and over mountains. They brought Chinese goods to the West. Many Europeans were fascinated with Chinese art and style. They especially liked the fine silk cloth. It was made from threads spun by silkworms.

The Silk Road was not a one-way road. Chinese products came out of China. And new ideas filtered into China along this road. Buddhism came to China from India in the second century A.D. In the next centuries it spread across China.

Mongol Invasion

To the north of China are the vast plains of central Asia. The people who lived there then were called Mongols. They were nomads, loosely organized into tribes. They wandered over their lands with their horses, sheep, camels, oxen, and goats. The Mongols were expert horsemen. And they were skilled at using the bow and arrow. In their camps they lived in felt tents called "yurts."

Genghis Khan

In A.D. 1206 a great chief took power over all the Mongols. His name was Genghis Khan. "Khan" was a title given to rulers. And Genghis Khan believed that he was destined to rule a great empire. He built up a huge army of Mongol soldiers. They conquered lands that included parts of China, Russia, Iran, and northern India. Genghis Khan had little education. But he was clever and ruthless. With his soldiers on horseback, he swept across the countryside. The thunder of the hooves of Mongol horses was a terrifying sound. The Mongols were among the most savage conquerors in history. If any city in their path tried to put up a fight, the Mongols showed no mercy. Every single person in the city would be killed.

Kublai Khan

Kublai Khan

Perhaps the greatest of the Khans was Kublai Khan. He was a grandson of Genghis Khan. Kublai Khan completed the conquest of China. Chinese farmers were no match for the Mongol armies. The Mongols ruled China from A.D. 1260 until A.D. 1368.

Marco Polo

Marco Polo was a trader and a traveler. He lived in Venice, Italy. Marco Polo traveled to China with his father and his uncle. They went to see Kublai Khan. His palace was in the capital city of Peking.

Kublai Khan welcomed the traders. He allowed Marco Polo to travel about his empire. The young Italian stayed in China for 17 years. Marco Polo saw sights that no other European had ever seen.

Then Marco Polo returned to Italy. He got caught up in a war. The fight was between Venice and another Italian city, Genoa. He was taken as a prisoner of war. He was thrown into jail in Genoa. There he told some amazing tales to a fellow prisoner who helped to write them down. The tales became a book, *Description of the World.* The book contained stories of the great Chinese civilization and of the empire of Kublai Khan.

Many people did not believe Marco Polo's tales. But the stories later proved to be true. He had written a good description of his adventures in China.

Marco Polo

Marco Polo and The Empire of Kublai Khan

Marco Polo found China a rich land. Kublai Khan ran his empire well. The emperor himself was a Buddhist. But he allowed religious freedom.

Kublai Khan gave Marco Polo permission to travel the country. Marco Polo found that travel in China was quite easy. Kublai Khan saw to it that roads were good and trips were pleasant. There were stones to mark the way. And trees were planted to give shade to travelers.

Kublai Khan developed a postal service. He wanted to make it easy for people throughout his empire to communicate. Horsemen carried messages along China's Great Wall. A post house stood every 25 miles along the wall. At each post house messengers could change horses. And travelers could rest. The Grand Canal was built to transport goods from north to south. Chinese boats called **junks** carried goods along the 850 miles of waterway.

Marco Polo was impressed with all he saw in China. The Chinese were using gunpowder and compasses. They used coal for heat. Marco Polo wrote that coal was "a sort of black stone, which they dig out of the mountainside. . . ." He was interested in their use of paper, especially for money. Europeans were still using heavy, metal coins.

Marco Polo's stories gave Europeans their first glimpse of life inside of China.

The End of Mongol Rule

In the 1300s the Chinese revolted against Mongol rule. It was the end of any foreign rule in China. The Mongols were driven away. The Ming dynasty reigned.

Ming emperors lived in Peking in a great palace known as the "Forbidden City." The Mings ruled there for nearly 300 years. Chinese art and literature thrived during this period. Europeans found Ming art beautiful. But the Chinese did not want European goods in trade. China would only accept payments of gold and silver.

Ming dynasty statuettes

In Japan . . .

Japan is a group of islands off the coast of China. Very little is known about the early history of Japan. Why? Because the ancient Japanese had no system of writing. Writing first came to Japan from China during the fifth century A.D. Customs, crafts, arts, and ideas of government and taxes also came to Japan from China. The Japanese adapted the Chinese calendar system and the ideas of Confucius. About A.D. 552 Buddhism came to Japan from China and Korea.

The Japanese visited China. The Chinese came to Japan. The Japanese began to model their way of life after the Chinese ways. In the seventh century one Japanese emperor was especially drawn to Chinese ways. He *ordered* changes in Japanese life to make it more like Chinese life.

Japan

Japan's Feudal System

Europeans of the Middle Ages lived under a system of feudalism. At the same time so did the Japanese. Japanese feudal society was divided into classes. Nobles were at the top. A class of warriors fought for the nobles. Japanese feudal warriors were called **samurai**. Samurai were given many privileges. The nobles gave them wealth and land. The samurai were respected as an upper class. In return, samurai warriors pledged loyalty and protection to their nobles.

The samurai were highly trained soldiers. They were expected to die, if necessary, for their noble. Samurai fought with huge, two-handed swords. Before attacking, a samurai would first shout his own name. Then he would shout of the bravery of his ancestors. This was meant to scare his enemy.

The nobles and samurai made up the upper classes of Japanese feudal society. But most of the population were peasants. They raised the food for the nobles and warriors.

Japanese society also included craftsmen and a few traders. Traders were looked down upon. Buying and selling goods was not considered honorable.

Samurai warrior, Japan

Feudal clans, or families, later united into larger groups. In time, Japan became a nation-state under one emperor. The emperor was called the Mikado. Japanese people honored their Mikado. But he had no real power. The country was actually ruled by a warlord, a military leader.

One of those warlords was a man called Yoritomo. In A.D. 1192 he began to use the title of "Shogun." This meant "great general." For almost 700 years one powerful shogun after another ruled Japan. Highly trained samurai enforced the shogun's rule. Shogun rule lasted until 1867.

Kublai Khan Faces the Samurai

Kublai Khan, the Mongol emperor, tried twice to conquer Japan. He launched attacks in 1274 and in 1281. Both times, his fleet was forced to flee because of a fierce storm. The Japanese called these raging storms "Kamikaze," or "Divine Wind."

Kublai Khan's fleet approaches Japan

The Hermit Nation

A **hermit** is someone who lives alone, away from others. Japan under the shoguns could be called a hermit nation. Japan showed little interest in the rest of the world. For years it remained isolated, like China.

The Italian traveler Marco Polo first told Europeans about Japan. He called the country Cipango, land of gold and riches. Europeans liked the sound of "gold and riches"! Traders began to travel to Japan.

At first the Japanese allowed the trade. They even welcomed Christian **missionaries**. But soon the shogun began to worry. He thought that Christianity and European ways might upset the Japanese culture. So the ruling shogun, of the Tokugawa family, closed the doors to Japan. Only the Dutch were allowed to continue a little trade. Just one Dutch ship a year could come to the port of Nagasaki.

The Japanese were strict about their rules. Stories tell of foreign sailors shipwrecked on Japanese shores being put to death. Their crime was that they had dared to set foot on Japanese soil!

The shogun also forbade the Japanese to travel outside of their country. Beginning in about 1600, Japan was totally separated from the rest of the world. For about the next 250 years, Japan remained alone.

In India . . .

For a long time India was divided into different kingdoms. Wealthy princes ruled each one. The people followed the Hindu religion. But in 273 B.C., Asoka became emperor. He converted to Buddhism. Most of India's people turned away from the Hindu religion with its strict caste laws. They turned to the gentler teachings of Buddha.

But later, the Hindu religion became popular in India again. Hindu believers flocked to the Ganges River to wash away their sins. The Hindus believed that all rivers came from the gods. They thought that the Ganges was especially holy.

The Moguls Invade India

In the eighth century A.D., Moslem warriors began a series of invasions into India.

The first Moslems came from Arabia. Three hundred years later, the invaders came from Persia and Afghanistan. The city of Delhi was captured several times. In 1206 Moslems set up a government in Delhi. Then in 1398 the conqueror Tamerlane and his army from central Asia raided India. Delhi was captured once again.

Mogul Rulers

In 1526 a Moslem prince of Afghanistan named Babar invaded India. He was a direct descendant of Genghis Khan. Babar conquered most of northern India. He established the Mogul empire and made himself emperor.

The greatest Mogul emperor was Babar's grandson, Akbar. He extended Mogul rule to most of India. He was a wise ruler. He was a Moslem. But he let others worship as they pleased. He tried to bring all religions together to live in harmony. Most of the empire remained Hindu.

The Mogul Empire lasted for about 200 years. These were good years. The strong central government provided a time of peace. The arts thrived. A special blend of Middle Eastern and Indian culture developed. The Moguls left fine buildings. One of these is the famous Taj Mahal. It was built by Shah Jahan as a tomb for his wife. Shah Jahan was the grandson of Akbar.

Shah Jahan had a son called Aurangzeb. In 1658 Aurangzeb took the throne. He threw his father in prison. Aurangzeb was a harsh ruler. He made Hindus pay a special tax. He destroyed many Hindu temples. He tried to force people to convert to Islam. In central India the Hindus revolted. The empire was weakened. Aurangzeb died in 1707. Shortly after, the Mogul Empire began to break up.

The Taj Mahal, Agra, India

In the Americas . . .

Until the end of the fifteenth century, most Europeans did not know about the Americas. Only the Vikings knew that land existed across the western sea. But one day the Europeans would call these lands the New World.

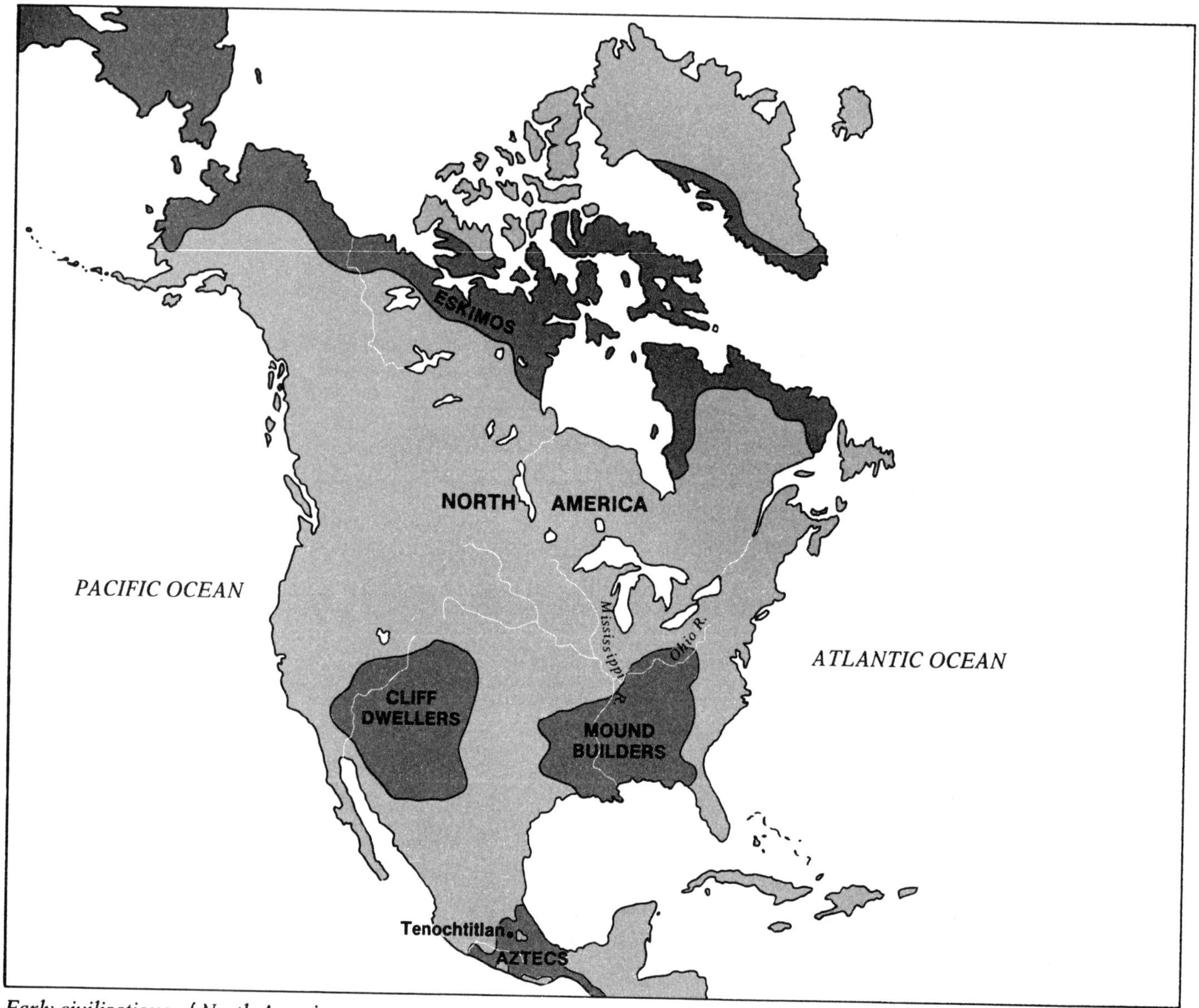

Early civilizations of North America

Mound Builders and Cliff Dwellers

Groups of Indians lived in different parts of the Americas. From about 100 B.C. to A.D. 500, the Hopewell Indians lived in the Ohio River Valley. They built huge burial mounds. As many as 1,000 people were sometimes buried in a single mound. Other Indians lived along the Mississippi River. They too built giant mounds of earth around A.D. 1000. They built their temples on top of the mounds. These Indians were called Mississippians. They lived mainly by farming.

To the west, in what is now New Mexico, Arizona, and Colorado, lived the cliff dwellers. These Indians were called Anasazi. The Anasazi are also called Pueblo Indians, from the Spanish word for "town." Around A.D. 1000 they began building villages on the sides of cliffs. All building was done with sandstone blocks and mud. Some homes were on protected ledges. Others were in hollow spaces in the cliff walls. Most homes were two or three stories high. As many as 1,500 people lived in one of these villages. But the Anasazi moved on by about A.D. 1300. By then their villages were empty. Perhaps the climate had become too dry to allow farming.

These Indians did not have a system of writing. What we know about them comes from the findings of archeologists.

Ancient cliff dwellings, Canyon de Chelly, Arizona

The Eskimos

Eskimos

Far north on the continent of North America lived the Eskimos. Eskimos ate the meat of caribou, seals, whales, and birds. They also ate fish from icy northern waters. They had no greens to eat. They got their vitamins by eating every part of an animal. They often ate the meat raw. The word "eskimo" is an American Indian word. It means "eater of raw meat." The Eskimos call themselves "Inuit," which means "people."

The Eskimos lived in one of the coldest places in the world. They made tools and weapons to fit their cold land. They traveled in sleds made of driftwood and leather. The sleds were pulled by teams of furry dogs. In the summer the Eskimos lived in tents made of animal skin. In winter they lived in houses made of blocks of snow. These houses were called "igloos."

Eskimos loved feasts and celebrations. Their medicine men danced and sang to the spirits of the earth and the air.

The first Europeans to meet Eskimos were the Vikings. Eskimos arrived in Greenland about A.D. 1100. They found Vikings living there.

The Aztecs

The Aztecs were another American Indian people. In the 1200s they settled in a large valley in Mexico. The Aztecs built one of the most advanced civilizations in the Americas.

"Find a place where a great eagle sits on a cactus," Aztec priests declared. "The eagle holds a snake in its beak. At that place you shall build your temple."

The Aztecs followed the words of their priests. They believed that these words came from the gods. So this is how they decided on a site for their capital. Where they found the eagle, they built the city of Tenochtitlan. Modern-day Mexico City is on the same site as Tenochtitlan, the ancient Aztec capital.

The Aztecs were a warlike people. They were feared by other Mexican tribes. During the 1400s, Aztec warriors conquered all the lands around Tenochtitlan. More conquests followed. Montezuma II came to the throne in 1502. He ruled the mighty Aztec empire from the capital city.

The Aztecs were always waging war. And they were always collecting tributes from those they conquered. The tributes came in the form of gold and silver, craftwork, food, and human prisoners. Young men and women were taken to the temples. They were offered as sacrifices to Aztec gods.

Human sacrifice was the worst part of Aztec civilization. The Aztec religion called for constant sacrifices to keep the gods happy. Aztec priests cut the hearts out of their living victims. They offered the hearts to the gods.

The Spanish explorer Hernando Cortez came to Tenochtitlan in 1519. He found an ugly sight. More than 100,000 skulls of the Aztecs' victims were displayed in a public square.

In spite of their cruel religious practices, the Aztecs had a well-ordered society. They invented a very simple form of picture writing. They also developed a system of numbers to help them keep track of what they owned. They had a calendar stone that recorded time. They built huge temples and buildings in a pyramid style.

Aztec pyramid, Mexico

Cortez conquers the Aztecs

The Aztecs had no need of money since they **bartered** for goods. Chocolate was a favorite drink. So cocoa beans were often traded. Our word "chocolate," in fact, comes from the Aztec language.

The Aztecs made some beautiful craftwork. Archeologists have found **mosaic** masks made of turquoise and jade. Aztecs also used colorful feathers to make headdresses and cloaks.

The Aztecs liked games and contests of athletic strength and skill. One of their favorite games was called "tlachiti." It was a combination of handball and basketball. The players had to put a very bouncy rubber ball through rings at either end of a court.

The Aztec empire came to a bloody end in 1521. Cortez and his army had arrived in Tenochtitlan in 1519. They were amazed at what they found. Tenochtitlan was larger than any Spanish city of that time. The Spaniards were welcomed in friendship. The Aztecs may have believed that Cortez was a long lost Aztec god. The god was supposed to have sailed away across the sea. And he was expected to return someday. But then Cortez captured the emperor, Montezuma, and made him a prisoner. The Aztecs rebelled in 1520 and drove the Spanish away. Montezuma died during the fighting. The next year Cortez returned and destroyed Tenochtitlan.

The Incas

The earliest history of the Incas is only legend. What we know for sure is that the Incas lived in the mountains of what is now South America's Peru. Around A.D. 1200 they began to spread out and build their empire. In time, the Incas conquered much of western South America. They took over the rest of Peru and parts of what is now Colombia, Bolivia, Ecuador, and Chile.

One man ruled the entire Inca Empire. He was called the Inca. His people worshiped him as a direct descendant of the sun. The sun was their most powerful god. The Inca's word was law. He had many officials to see that his laws were obeyed.

The Inca ruled over a giant empire from his capital at Cuzco. More than 6 million people lived under his rule. Communicating with all these subjects was a problem. So the Incas built a fine network of roads. These roads connected all corners of the empire. The Incas also built bridges of twisted vines to stretch across steep jungle ravines. They had no horses or wheeled vehicles. All traveling was done on foot. Llamas carried their goods.

Swift runners raced along the Inca roads to deliver messages. The Incas had no system of writing. So messages were passed by word of mouth. Runners also carried "quipus." These were different colored ropes with knots to stand for numbers. They used the quipus to keep track of things.

The Inca Empire

Ruins of Machu Picchu, Peru

The Incas built rest stops along their roads. At each stop a tired runner could tell his message to a fresh runner. Then that messenger would hurry to the next stop. This relay system kept communication moving across the empire.

Ancient Inca stone walls, Cuzco, Peru

Ancient Inca statuette, Peru

The Incas were fine builders. They used huge stone blocks. They fit the blocks together very carefully. They needed no mortar or cement of any kind. Some of the stones fit together so tightly that the blade of a knife cannot slide between them! Inca buildings still stand at Cuzco today, even after earthquakes have destroyed modern structures.

The Incas had plenty of gold and plenty of silver. Their temples were decorated with both of the valuable metals. Inca artists made beautiful objects of solid gold. These were often inlaid with precious jewels.

It is no wonder that the Spanish explorers were drawn to the Incas. In 1532 tales of great wealth brought Francisco Pizarro to South America. His visit was the beginning of the end of the Inca civilization.

Two Worlds Meet

For centuries the rest of the world did not know about the Americas or the people living there. Then the Vikings landed in North America. But they left no lasting colonies. Much later, European explorers found the continent by accident. What they were really looking for was a quicker route to India and the Far East. The place they found seemed like a land of wealth and plenty. It seemed well worth exploring and conquering. The next chapter in world history would be an exciting time of exploration and discovery.

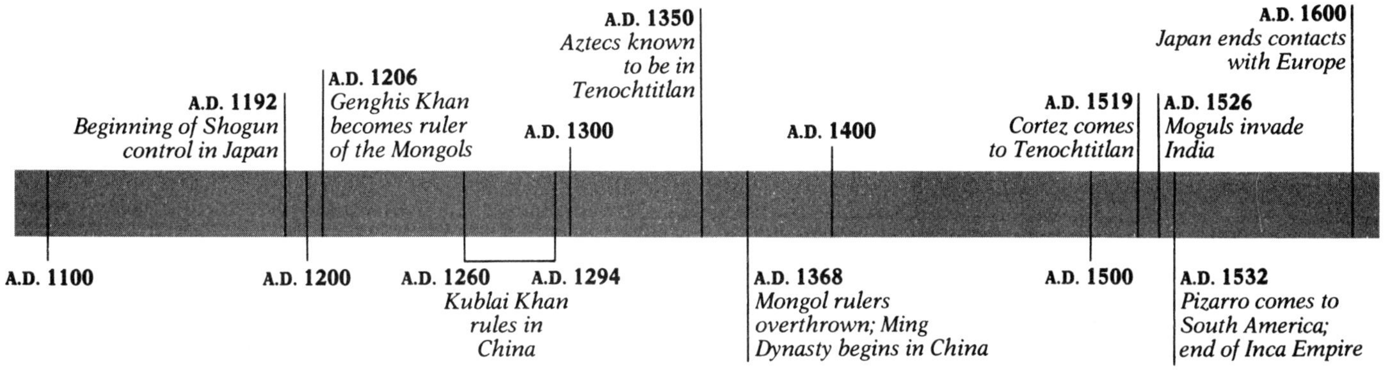

Points to Remember

- ◆ The Great Wall of China, mountains, and deserts all helped to isolate China from the rest of the world.
- ◆ Confucius taught the Chinese to honor their families, respect their ancestors, and value education.
- ◆ The Chinese used paper, printing, and gunpowder long before the Europeans did.
- ◆ Mongols from the north invaded China and ruled an empire there for nearly 100 years.
- ◆ Marco Polo, an Italian trader, visited China and took home stories of his travels.
- ◆ The Japanese lived under a feudal system similar to the one in Europe.
- ◆ The samurai were Japanese warriors, and shoguns were ruling warlords.
- ◆ In the early 1600s Japan's shogun forbade travel and trade outside Japan.
- ◆ Moslem invaders brought the Moslem religion to India.
- ◆ Until the late 1400s most Europeans did not know that the Americas existed.
- ◆ The Aztecs developed a large, warlike civilization in Mexico.
- ◆ The Incas made their homes in the mountains of Peru.
- ◆ The Incas' empire spread throughout much of western South America. It was linked by a fine system of roads and bridges.

Think About It!

1. What "rule to live by" did Confucius teach the Chinese people?
2. Following Confucius's teachings, how did the Chinese choose their government officials?
3. Why did the shoguns forbid trade outside of Japan?
4. How did the Mogul emperors treat Indians who were not Moslems?
5. Why did certain groups of North American Indians build giant mounds?
6. Why did the Aztecs sacrifice human beings?
7. Why were the Spaniards so interested in the Incas and their South American lands?

A Pacemaker® Book

SIMON & SCHUSTER

FEARON/JANUS/QUERCUS
Supplementary Education Group

TP
APEX
9780822474753